Margaret A. Rice

September 29th 2022

THE HENRY BAGWELL STORY

English Adventurer, Virginia Planter
1589–1663

MARGARET A. RICE

The Henry Bagwell Story: English Adventurer,
Virginia Planter (1589–1663)

For information about this title, contact the publisher:
Secant Publishing, LLC
615 North Pinehurst Avenue
Salisbury MD 21801 USA
www.secantpublishing.com

ISBN: 978-1-944962-84-5 (hardcover)
ISBN: 978-1-944962-85-2 (ebook)
Library of Congress Control Number: 2020915742

To M.K. Miles, Co-creator with the late Barry W. Miles of the genealogy database "Miles Files"

and

The Brooks Miles Barnes Archives Room at the Eastern Shore Regional Library and Heritage Center, Parksley, Virginia

CONTENTS

ILLUSTRATIONS

Front Cover: Colonists on their way to Virginia (from *Bideford Trade Maps* by Maggie Curtis, 2019).

1.1 St. Petrock's Church. Courtesy of Russ Liley, Freeline Graphics, Exeter. (p. 19)

1.2 Johane Chappell's record of birth. Dymond's Notebooks, Chapple Family files, SWHT, Exeter (p. 21)

1.3 David Bagwell's death record. St. Olave's Church records, SWHT. (p. 23)

1.4 David Bagwell, a page from the inventory. Courtesy of Exeter City Council. (p. 25)

1.5 A Tudor house in Exeter. By John Olney, courtesy of Maria Olney. (p. 26)

2.1 A bench end at St. Mary's Church, East Budleigh, Devon, depicting an Early Tudor Ship. (p. 31)

5.1 The *Deliverance*, a reconstruction of the seventeenth-century ship at Ordnance Island, St. George's, in Bermuda. (p. 64)

6.1 Jamestown Memorial Church. Courtesy of Jamestown Rediscovery Foundation (Preservation Virginia). Photo by Chuck Durfor. (p. 80)

8.1 Map of the Eastern Shore. From Whitelaw, Ralph Thomas, *Virginia's Eastern Shore* (Virginia Historical Society, 1951), p. 16. By permission of Virginia Museum of History and Culture. (p. 112)

8.2 Original court record, 1633, showing the signatures of Obedience Robins and Henry Bagwell. From the original held at Northampton County Court: Order Book No. 1, 1633, Courtesy of Northampton County Court, Bayside Transcriptions. (p. 115)

Epilogue

Appendices

Foreword

The Henry Bagwell Story is an honest and thorough investigation of the life and times of a significant individual in the history of early America. Although Henry Bagwell's name is not a household word, it deserves a place in the story of our seventeenth-century origins. He was a survivor in the early Chesapeake Bay region at a time when hundreds were dying soon after their arrival in the New World. Not only did he live through a very important time in the development of the Virginia colony, he was an active participant. As first clerk of the court of "ye Kingdom of Accawamacke" on the Eastern Shore, he was instrumental in writing the history of his time. He had the opportunity and obligation to record the events which were at the very core of the early Virginia settlement. These records are the oldest continuous records in English-speaking America, and even yet, they have not been mined as thoroughly as they should be to inform the history of the period. Secondly, as a member of the House of Burgesses meeting in Jamestown, he witnessed, and participated in, the contentious discussion around some of the pivotal acts that led to representative government in America.

M.A. Rice has admirably succeeded in letting the records speak for themselves, leaving out the twenty-first century prejudices that all-too-frequently plague histories written today. She has neither tried to glorify nor vilify Bagwell. Rather, she has gleaned from the extant record the story of an individual who helped to build America. This story could be—and should be—replicated many times to bring to life other early settlers and their contributions in constructing this New World settlement in the Chesapeake. She has also delved into the English background of Bagwell, showing how over several generations the Bagwell family became a productive part of England's way of life. This is local history at its best—told in a straightforward way. Hopefully this monograph will spawn similar efforts, which, building-block-like, will lead to a more complete depiction of Virginia's early settlement period. Each person who came to the Chesapeake in 1607 played a role that needs to be examined. As more and more of these mini-histories are recounted, a more complete and accurate understanding of early American will emerge.

As a student of the colonial Chesapeake, I have long hoped that historians would pull from the records those individual stories, each of which tells an important part about the origins and development of our country. History is the story of people and their undertakings, their hopes and aspirations. Rice has followed the suggestion of historian James Perry, whose *Formation of a Society on Virginia's Eastern Shore, 1615–1655,* shows how original sources can further our understanding of a period. Bagwell's life is one of these stories—consisting of wide-ranging seventeenth-century political and legal enactments, economic growth and transformation, diverse social interactions, and religious life in a frontier society, separated by thousands of miles from the mother country and its institutions. Through this, we come to see a man and the society of which he was a productive part. I commend Ms. Rice for her diligent and thorough research in creating a readable and accurate account.

Rice has traced Bagwell's life from his English origins in the south western county of Devon through his immigration to Jamestown, fraught with many difficulties on the transatlantic voyage, to his early years in Virginia and his eventual settling on the Eastern Shore of Virginia. She has given us a broad panorama as well as the close-up picture of a family and its trials and triumphs during the first decades of settlement in Virginia. Although Rice started this project as a family history, it has turned into much more than just a genealogical record. Bagwell and members of his family are described in as much detail as the surviving legal, land, probate, vital, and religious records will allow. Researchers of Eastern Shore history and its people will find this a worthwhile read. I suspect Henry Bagwell, if he had had the opportunity to read this work, would recognize himself in the political, economic, and social interactions of the time.

G. Ray Thompson, PhD

Professor of History Emeritus
Co-Founder, Nabb Research Center for Delmarva History and
Culture
Salisbury University

Introduction

This unprecedented flow of colonists and adventurers included prominent individuals whose names made their way into the colony's official records. However, the majority — the ordinary men, women, and children, whose efforts enabled the colony to become viable — simply escaped notice. As a result, 400 years later we still yearn to know about Virginia's earliest settlers.

Martha McCartney, *Virginia Immigrants and Adventurers*[1]

The first clerk of the Accomack Plantation in Virginia, according to extant records, was Henry Bagwell, who continued to serve in that capacity for several years after the Plantation was made a county. But "Little is known about his life prior to arrival in Accomack,"[2] according to Susie M. Ames, founder and second president of the Eastern Shore Historical Association.

My aim in this book is to provide evidence of Henry Bagwell's life from the city of his birth, in Exeter, Devon, in the South West of England, to the Eastern Shore of Virginia, where he settled and made a life with his family.

I wish to celebrate the life of a remarkable man.

Henry Bagwell was born in Devon in 1589, the second son of

---

1   McCartney, Martha W., *Virginia Immigrants and Adventurers, 1607–1635* (Baltimore, Genealogical Publishing Company, 2007), p. 9.

2   Ames, Susie M., *County Court Records of Accomack-Northampton, 1632–1640* (Washington, The American Historical Association, 1954), Introduction, p. xv.

David Bagwell, merchant of Exeter, and the grandson of Thomas Chappell, merchant, alderman, and mayor of Exeter in 1588.

Henry was one of those earliest settlers who chose to leave England and seek the opportunities of a new life in the New World. Many of those who made the same choice as Henry were lost on the long sea voyages across the Atlantic, or died of hunger and disease during the first years of living in a new and challenging environment. The early governors are well known—the men appointed by the Virginia Company of London to govern the new colony. Others who made an impact on events are also recorded. These include John Rolfe, who married Pocahontas, daughter of the local Native American leader Powhatan, and who also discovered the strain of tobacco that gave the colony a successful export crop and financial security; and Sir George Yeardley, who led the convening of the first Assembly in Jamestown in 1619.

Another well-documented event was the sailing of the Third Supply, a fleet of ships led by the *Sea Venture*, commissioned by the Virginia Company of London in 1609 to take urgent supplies and more colonists to rescue Jamestown, England's first permanent colony in the New World. Henry Bagwell was one of the passengers on the *Sea Venture*, which became separated from the fleet in a huge storm and was wrecked on the island of Bermuda. The passengers survived for nine months and built two smaller pinnaces, the *Patience* and *Deliverance*, in which they continued their voyage, finally reaching Virginia in May 1610.

Henry is one of those ordinary men who survived and went on to own land in one of the new settlements; he survived the early years of the colony and became a planter, a burgess, and clerk of the first County Court of Northampton, a vestryman, and tobacco inspector, and was nominated for the role of sheriff.

We follow in his footsteps as he leaves his home city of Exeter to travel to Virginia's Eastern Shore. He made a successful transition from the Old World to the New.

This is one man's personal story of adventure, who survived, succeeded, and played a small part in the history of Virginia; a family man whose life and those of his children can be traced in the old records of Virginia which, with other records, have provided evidence of the life and times of one pioneer family.

Henry did not leave a will and the place of his burial has still not been found.

He left land and property to his two sons, John and Thomas Bagwell, which was witnessed in the court records of Accomack-Northampton. John and Thomas, in turn, were able to pass the land on to the next generation and this was verified in their wills.

Henry's sons and daughters married into the other pioneer families of the Eastern Shore and many of his descendants remain on the Eastern Shore, while others migrated to different areas of the United States.

Henry's story emerged in Devon while I was researching my family history. My uncle left me a hand-drawn family tree tracing our line back to Thomas Chappell, and he was my starting point. Thomas and his wife Thomazine were married in 1565, and had ten children: John, born in 1566, Johane in 1568, William in 1569, Nicholas in 1571, and six others. Johane married David Bagwell in 1586 and was the mother of Henry Bagwell and six other children. Her younger brother, Nicholas Chappell, was my ancestor. Consequently, Henry Bagwell must be accounted a relative of mine.

More than four centuries later, I have undergone my own voyage of discovery, tracing his footsteps across the Atlantic from Devon to the Eastern Shore of Virginia.

Margaret A. Rice

Part I

TRANSITION

Chapter 1
Henry Bagwell's Origins in Devon

Henry Bagwell was born in October 1589 in the city of Exeter, the cultural and industrial center of the county of Devon in the South West of England, during the reign of Queen Elizabeth I.

Henry's father was David Bagwell who, in 1585, had become an apprentice to Thomas Chappell, a rich merchant, alderman, and mayor of Exeter. His mother was Johane Chappell, the eldest daughter of Thomas and Thomazine Chappell. She was one of ten children born to Thomas and Thomazine in the city and christened in the ancient church of St. Petrock (see Figure 1.1) in the parish of St. Petrock,[1] one of sixteen parish churches within the enclosure of the walled city of Exeter. The city's significant features included a castle built by William the Conqueror, a Bishop's Palace, an ancient Guildhall on the High Street, the Cathedral of St. Peter with its west front of carved medieval statues, a ship canal built in

Figure 1.1 St.Petrock's Church. Courtesy of Russ Liley, Freeline Graphics, Exeter.

---

1 St. Petrock's Parish Records. Transcribed by Reverend F. Nesbitt (DCRS at SWHT).

1566, and many houses of the rich and successful merchants of the city.

As a result of his marriage to Johane Chappell, David moved into the circle of one of the leading merchant families of Tudor Exeter. He was admitted to the Liberties of the city and made a freeman in 1585. This enabled him to set up in business in his own right as merchant and apprentice to Thomas Chappell, which was confirmed in the court records of November 1585–1586.[2]

Thomas and his brother William were members of a vibrant merchant community with new guilds emerging to support and protect the rights of merchants. Exeter was at the very center of the trade in wool, its merchants made rich by the trading opportunities with France and Spain. The cloth merchants had acquired a chapel in 1471, which they altered to create Tuckers Hall, where the Guild of Weavers, Tuckers and Shearmen met to regulate the growing business of the cloth trade. In 1564 they had been granted a coat of arms which showed a weaver's shuttle, burling irons, a teasel frame, and a pair of shears.

Another strong guild in Exeter was the Society of Merchant Adventurers, which had been established in 1560 and supported the merchants who bought and sold cloth in France, Spain, and other areas in Europe. William Chappell, the older brother of Thomas, was one of the first members of this society.

Exeter also had a strong civic organization with control vested in a group of men known as the Twenty-four, who elected the mayor and other officials from their number and were agents of the Crown. William and Thomas Chappell were aldermen, members, and governors of the guilds, and both held the powerful role of mayor, William

---

2 Rowe, Margery M. and Jackson, Andrew M., *Exeter Freemen, 1266–1967, Mayor's Court Book 55* (Exeter, DCRS, Extra Series, No. 1, 1973), p. 99.

in 1569 and 1579, and Thomas in 1588.[3] Thomas was also a church-warden at St. Petrock's Church in 1574, governor of the Merchant Adventurers in 1585, and sheriff in 1586.

David Bagwell was part of this family and, as the son-in-law of Thomas Chappell, would have been able to take advantage of their links with other merchant families and the civic authorities.

1.2 Johane Chappell's record of birth. Dymond's Notebooks, Chapple Family files. SWHT.

3   Oliver, Reverend George, *The History of the City of Exeter* (Exeter, William Roberts, 1861), p. 232.

In 1586 David and Johane were living in the parish of St. Petrock, most probably in the home of the Chappell family. David's tax assessment in 1586 indicated that he contributed £4 4s. in goods to the Subsidy.[4] When Thomas Chappell died in 1589 his house was described in an inventory of his estate.[5] It was a large house with three floors, a cellar, a shop and warehouse, a counting house, a barn with wheat, rye, and beans, and large enough to accommodate some pigs, sheep, and two horses. The rooms were filled with fine furniture with wall hangings, curtains for the windows, feather beds, and curtains for the beds. There were cupboards where his gilt tankards, bowls, salt pots, and silver spoons could be stored.

The first three children of David and Johane were christened in St. Petrock's Church: William on 23 July 1587, Priscilla on 27 September 1588, and Henry on 29 October 1589.[6]

At some point the family moved to the parish of St. Mary Arches, and there is a record that David paid taxes of £6 in goods to the Subsidy of 1593/5.[7] Four more children were christened in St. Mary Arches Church: John in 1592, Andrew in 1593, Elizabeth in 1596, and Davy in 1597.[8]

Early deaths and the Orphan's Court

Thomas Chappell died early, leaving a young family. Queen Elizabeth I had established Orphans' Courts to note the assets of children under 21 years of age who had been orphaned by the early death of a rich father. The court authorized inventories to be taken by assessors who recorded in great detail the contents of the houses,

---

4   Rowe, Margery, M. (ed.), *Tudor Exeter, Tax assessments, 1489–1595, including the Military Survey, 1522* (Exeter, DCRS, New Series, Vol. 2, 1977), p. 71.

5   Thomas Chappell, Inventory: Original, ECA 43 (SWHT); Crocker, Jannine, *Elizabethan Inventories and Wills of Exeter's Orphans' Court*, Vol. 1 and 2 (Exeter, DCRS, 2016), p. 232.

6   St. Petrock's Parish Records, Nesbitt.

7   Rowe, *Tudor Exeter, Tax assessments, 1489–1595*, p. 76.

8   St. Mary Arches Parish Records. Transcribed by C.A.T. Fursdon (DCRS at SWHT).

1.3 David Bagwell's death record. St. Olave's Church records, SWHT.

properties, and leases, with a value attached to each item within their houses. Exeter's first chamberlain, John Hooker, was responsible for recording the decisions of the Exeter Orphans' Court, which were set down in one of his Act Books.[9] Thomas Chappell also left an individual will.

When Thomas died in 1589, he left a large inheritance to his family, £3,225 with £1,303 in money at his house.[10] He left £150 to each of his nine youngest children who were under 21.

His oldest daughter, Johane Bagwell, also received this amount, two silver spoons, and a silver goblet with gilt. In his will Thomas named in addition his son-in-law, David Bagwell, and their two oldest children, William and Priscilla:

> I remite to Dauid Bagwell my sonn-in-law Twenty pondes of lawful money of Englande wch he oweth me. Geue vnto the forsoad Daiuid Bagwills Children called William and Presylla and to euely of them. The some of three [pounds].[11]

William and Henry Bagwell, as sons of a successful merchant of Exeter, would have attended the High School, the only grammar school in the city,[12] whose students usually went on to be apprentices for seven years with a master. William and Henry would have moved into the family business as an equivalent to an apprenticeship.

In 1603, Henry's father died on a voyage to Brittany. The records of St. Olave's Church stated: "Bagwell, David, Mrchaunte, Dyed beyond the seas and buried 1603."[13] It was noted that he died in St. Malo, Brittany.[14]

---

9   Hooker, John, *The Act Books*, Vol. II to VIII (1508–1640).

10 Hoskins, W.G., *Old Devon* (London, David and Charles, 1966), pp. 78–81.

11 Thomas Chappell, Inventory: Original, ECA 43 (SWHT); Crocker, *Inventories*, p. 230.

12 Hoskins, *Old Devon*, p. 83.

13 St. Olave's Parish Records. Transcribed by C.A.T. Fursdon and E. Serle (1937, DRCS at SWHT).

14 Hoskins, *Old Devon*, p. 77.

1.4 David Bagwell, a page from the inventory. Courtesy of Exeter City Council.

David's inventory for the Orphans' Court has provided an accurate description of the house where Henry Bagwell spent his early years.[15]

There is a description of the merchandise in his shop and warehouse and evidence of his father's trading activities. Henry may have worked with him in the family shop, or in the warehouse or may have travelled with him on trading visits to France.

15 David Bagwell, Inventory: Original, ECA 179 (SWHT).

Henry's first home

According to the description detailed for the Orphans' Court, the house had a hall, the main room of the house, where the family would have met to eat their food; it had a table, one large chair, eight lower stools, and three low chairs. There was a chest, cupboard, and a table inscribed with figures from the story of Troy.

Figure 1.5 A Tudor house in Exeter. By John Olney, courtesy of Maria Olney.

There was a little parlor with a small table and a large cupboard with doors. In the kitchen was a fireplace where logs could be burned with dog-bars to support the logs. There was a good selection of cooking utensils: one described as a "skynker" (a kind of flagon), skillets, cauldrons (large containers for hot liquids suspended over a fire), copper kettles, brass ladles, iron pots, and chaffing dishes (used with a chaffer—a small enclosed brazier containing hot coals for heating food). There were wooden benches with high backs, a wooden table and benches, a chair and two stools, brass and tin candlesticks, little pots, and a salt cellar.

Another room above the kitchen had a feather bed and pillows, another bed named a "dustbed" (a mattress filled with chaff or flock), and another called a "standing bed" with a truckle bed underneath. There were blankets and colored covers, a chest, small stools, and a "lokinge Glasse." Another bedroom over the parlor had a feather bed and a truckle bed with a cover of tapestry as well as a painted cloth on the walls.

In the house were also a "meal chamber" for the preparation of food and a "bake chamber" for the baking of food. A gallery contained linen tablecloths, curtains, cushions, cloth for wall hangings, and weapons—muskets, pistols, a pike, and a halberd (a military weapon combining a spear and battle axe on a handle 5 to 7 feet long).

Outside was a stable and courtyard where there was a cistern of lead covered with timber (used for brewing or perhaps the main household water container), washing tubs, glass, and casements for windows.

The warehouse

Henry's father was a mercer and dealt with a trade of fine textile fabrics. The range of goods he left behind was described in detail in the inventory and provided the evidence of his overseas trade. These included: cambric, a white linen made at Cambrai, France; cruell, a thin worsted yarn of two threads, used in tapestry and embroidery; dimmed, a stout cloth used for bed curtains; dornexe, fabric originally manufactured at Doornick, a Flemish town, and used in hangings and carpets; Holland, a linen fabric originally named after the province of Holland in the Netherlands; mockadowe, woollen cloth used in clothing; an imitation velvet, sometimes called mock velvet; cushions, silk thread, silver and silk buttons, woollen hose for women, coloured fringes, and a bag of alum, used for dyeing and tawing (a method of tanning skins). There was also a hogshead of cider and some coarse French wool. The most expensive items were pieces of Normandy canvas. Also noted was an item of methernexe, a type of canvas in Dartmouth, a busy port in South Devon which imported and exported cloth at this time.

Other property and settlements

David had owned another house in Exeter, leased out to Mrs. Jurden (Jurdaine) in Northgate Street in Exeter, valued at £10 10s., and a stable in St. Mary's Arches Lane, valued at 8s. This would have brought additional money into the family. Another small house in the city was noted and a house in the country where he had sheep, milking cows, two horses, pigs, and seven acres of wheat and rye. There was a stable and hay loft. He leased out some of the ground, valued at £10. He also owned the glass and casement fitting for a tenement in Boucher (Butcher) Row.

A statement in the inventory said that David died on December 13, 1603, and noted that Henry's mother, Johane Bagwell, received compensation for David's death. There was an additional item in the inventory:

> Item she sayeth she hathe Received from St Mallas [St. Malo] sisthence the death of her husband in moneyey more in moneyey

she saye the xxxxvi xvii [£46 17s.], and two peeces of Fyne Beadwoerke, valued at £8 6s. 8d.

Henry also received money and was named in the inventory. He was owed £12 from his father's estate. When Henry's father died he was in debt and, in a list of merchants' estates, this was given as debts of £777.[16] William, as the oldest son, would have inherited his father's business and assets. He moved to the port town of Topsham on the River Exe and founded his own family. In 1609 Johane Bagwell married John Parr, another rich merchant of Exeter, who would have taken over the care of the younger children.

A voyage to Virginia, 1609

In May, Henry was a passenger on the *Sea Venture*, the flagship of a fleet known as the Third Supply on its voyage to Virginia. Henry was 20 years of age, and one of 150 passengers on the ship, with other gentlemen and women, soldiers, and seamen who sought new opportunities and adventure offered by the Virginia Company of London. This large fleet of nine ships had been brought together to take more supplies and more than 500 new colonists to replace those lost in the first two years of establishing England's first permanent colony in the New World.

16 Hoskins, *Old Devon*, p. 78.

Chapter 2

The Early Explorers of Virginia and the Challenges of 1606–1609

Setting the scene: The first explorers, 1578–1603

Many Devon explorers had been involved in the expeditions to discover new lands. Sir Walter Raleigh was a Devon man, born around 1552 at Hayes Barton in the village of East Budleigh. He was the son of Walter Raleigh and Katherine (widow of Otho Gilbert), and served in France and the Netherlands. Katherine was buried in the ancient church of All Saints at East Budleigh, where Walter Raleigh Senior was a churchwarden. In 1578, Sir Humphrey Gilbert, Walter Raleigh's half-brother, had been issued a six-year patent by Queen Elizabeth I, which gave him the rights to explore the North American coast and plant colonies in areas not already claimed by other European powers, as well as search for a North West passage to the Far East. On Gilbert's first voyage, Raleigh captained the *Falcon* with Simon Fernandez as master. This voyage failed, but Gilbert's second voyage in 1583 established a settlement at St. John's in Newfoundland. Tragically Gilbert drowned on his way back to England.

Raleigh, now a favored courtier, petitioned the Queen to take over Gilbert's patent and was successful. A patent was confirmed and signed by Sir John Popham, the Attorney General, in March 1584. This confirmed Raleigh's right to explore new lands on behalf of the Queen.

By April 1584, Raleigh had sponsored the first reconnaissance voyage to North America with Captain Philip Amadas and Arthur Barlowe. They travelled through the Canary Islands and West Indies, arriving on the coast of North America on July 4, and claimed the land for England. They discovered Roanoke Island and returned to England with two Native Americans, Manteo and Wanchese. Raleigh was knighted; the Queen allowed him to use the name Virginia (instead of Wingandacoa) for the land and named him governor.

2.1 A bench end at All Saints Church, East Budleigh, Devon, depicting an Early Tudor Ship.

Raleigh sponsored a second voyage in 1585, with seven ships, led by the *Tiger*, which was captained by Sir Richard Grenville, an experienced seaman from the port of Bideford in North Devon.[1] On this voyage were Ralph Lane, whom Raleigh had appointed to be the governor of the intended colony on Roanoke, Thomas Harriot, who was a scientist, and John White, an artist, whose drawings provided the first view of the life of the Native Americans of the area and local plants and animals. Governor Lane organized the building of a small fort on Roanoke Island.

Grenville left for England on 25 August 1585 and, on his way back to Bideford, he captured a Spanish treasure ship, the *Santa Maria de San Vincente*.

1   Nicholls, Mark, and Williams, Penry. *Sir Walter Raleigh: In Life and Legend* (London, Bloomsbury, 2011), p. 51.

He returned to Bideford with a Native American, who was baptized in St. Mary's Church, Bideford, but died the next year. The following entries are from the church register:

> 1588, Christnynge Raleigh, a Wynganditoia, baptised 27th of March
>
> 1589, Buryinge, Rawly, a man of Wynganditoia on the day of Aprill-four [2]

Lane, Harriot, and White explored the area and gained important information about the land from the Native Americans they met during these explorations.

During one exploration up the Roanoke river, Lane became aware of rumors being spread by Pemisapan (previously known as Wingina), the chief of Native Americans on Roanoke Island. These rumors had been spread to the other local tribes, and indicated that the English were planning to attack them. [3]

The relationship between the English and the Native Americans had deteriorated after the death in 1586 of Pemisapan's father, Ensenore, who had protected the English settlers. Both the English and the Native Americans were fearful of an attack, and Pemisapan decided to leave Roanoke Island. The Native Americans did not sow any corn, with the hope that the English would have no source of food and would starve.

White decided to organize a surprise attack, which resulted in the death of Pemisapan:

> On 1 June, at the watchword "Christ our victory" the settlers shot the king and his "chief men," giving them in Lane's words "that which they had purposed for us." After falling, Pemisapan

---

2 Rogers, Inkerman, *A Concise History of Bideford, AD 878–1936* (Bideford, 1938), p. 12.

3 Nicholls and Williams, *Sir Walter Raleigh*, p. 54.

got up and fled into the woods, where he was pursued by one of Lane's men, who returned with the chief's head in his hand.[4]

Grenville had not yet returned with supplies, and continued hostilities with the Native Americans made life very difficult for the men at the fort on this small settlement.

Sir Walter Raleigh had also asked Sir Francis Drake, on his return from a privateering mission, to visit Roanoke with supplies for the colonists. However, the poor relationship with the Native Americans and lack of food and supplies had convinced Ralph Lane that they should abandon the colony. He left three men on the island and he and all the other colonists left in June, returning to England with Drake. Another supply ship sent by Raleigh arrived but found the colony deserted and so went back to England. When Grenville finally arrived with supplies 15 days later, he also found the colony deserted, and left 15 men to hold the fort in the name of England.[5]

Raleigh's third attempt was in 1587, led by John White. This is from White's narrative of the 1587 voyage:

> In the yeere of our Lorde, 1587 Walter Ralegh intending to persevere in the planting of his Countrey of Virginia, prepared a new Colonies of one hundred and fiftie men to be sent thither, under the charge of John White, whom he appointed Governour, and also appointed unto him twelve Assistants, unto whome he gave a Charter, and incorporated them by the name of the Governour, and Assistants of the Citie of Ralegh, in Virginia.[6]

The colonists included "seventeen women and nine children against eight-six men,"[7] including White's own daughter, Elinor, wife of

---

4   Ibid.

5   From Richard Hakluyt's "Narratives of the 1586 Virginia Voyages," in: Quinn, David. B and Quinn, Alison (eds.), *The First Colonists* (North Carolina, Archives and History, North Carolina Department of Cultural Resources, 2007), p. 86.

6   From John White's narrative of the 1587 Virginia voyage, in: Quinn, *First Colonists*, p. 93.

7   Nicholls and Williams, *Sir Walter Raleigh*, p. 59.

Ananias Dare. On August 18, notes White:

> Elenora, daughter to the Governour and wife of one of the
> Assistants, was delivered of a daughter in Roanoak, and the
> same day was christened there the Sunday following and
> because she was the first Christian borne in Virginia, she was
> named Virginia.[8]

The colonists set about mending houses and settling in to their new
environment, but the lack of food and equipment and other supplies
made life difficult, and they persuaded Governor White to return to
England. On 27 August he prepared to leave, arriving in Ireland in
October, and finally in England, as White recounts: "November 5
the Governour landed in England at Martasew, neere Saint Michaels
Mount in Cornwall."[9]

White would never see his daughter and granddaughter again.

In 1588, Sir Richard Grenville prepared another fleet to return
to Virginia with more colonists and supplies. Orders came from the
Privy Council in London which instructed him instead to take his
ships to join with the fleet at Plymouth, preparing to attack the
Spanish Armada. White was desperate to return to Virginia and
managed to obtain two small pinnaces, the *Brave* and the *Roe*. Sadly
this voyage was doomed to disaster, with storms and attacks from
privateers, as White recounts: "On 22 of May we came to an anker
betweene Lunday and Harting point neere unto Clavell key where
we road until the next tyde, and thence we put over the barre, and
the same day landed at Biffeford."[10]

Finally on August 15, 1590, three years after his departure, White
arrived at what we now call the Outer Banks. The next morning the
English saw what they presumed to be a signal from the colonists,

---

8   From John White's narrative of the 1587 Virginia voyage, in: Quinn, *First Colonists*, p. 102.
9   Ibid., p. 106.
10   From John White's narrative of the abortive 1588 Virginia voyage, in: Quinn, *First Colonists*, p. 114.

but after a long walk down the beach they found no settlers. On August 18, 1590, Virginia Dare's birthday, the English finally arrived at the site of the village. They found carved on the palisade the word "CROATOAN" without any crosses or signs of distress.[11] White had left instructions with the settlers to carve a cross if they had been in danger. He tried to travel to the area known as Croatoan, but was unable to reach it due to stormy weather. He returned to England, arriving in Plymouth in October 1590. These settlers became known as the "Lost Colony."

In 1603 Raleigh sent Bartholomew Gilbert to Chesapeake Bay to establish a colony and search for the lost colonists, but Gilbert and his men were attacked by the Algonquian Indians. Gilbert was killed and the survivors returned to England, but Raleigh did not lose his ambition of returning to the New World.

The challenges of establishing a permanent colony, 1606–1608

James I had become king on the death of Elizabeth I in 1603, and, in 1606, a group of merchants and men involved in the civic world of London and Plymouth asked the king for a charter to continue the colonization of America. The first charter was granted on April 10, 1606 to the newly formed Virginia Company of London, and established two separate companies, one based in London with city merchants, knights, and adventurers, and the other based in the South West with merchants and adventurers of Plymouth. Each company was allocated a designated area along the coast of America: the London Company would explore the southern region, and the Plymouth Company the northern regions.

The London Company was the first to organize an expedition and,

---

11 Fort Raleigh National Historic Park, North Carolina. www.nps.gov.fora.

on December 20, 1606, Captain Christopher Newport led a small fleet of three ships, headed by his vessel, the *Susan Constant*; the *Godspeed*, commanded by Captain Bartholomew Gosnold; and *Discovery*, captained by John Ratcliffe. Among the list of gentlemen on board were Edward Maria Wingfield, Captain John Smith, Captain George Kendall, Captain John Martin, Robert Hunt, a preacher, George Percy, Anthony Gosnold (brother of Bartholomew), and Captain Gabriell Archer. Many of these men were to play a decisive role in the founding of Virginia. There were twenty-four other men classified as gentlemen; two surgeons, named as Thomas Wotton and William Wilkinson; four carpenters, William Laxon, Edward Pising, Thomas Emry, and Robert Small; twelve laborers; two bricklayers, William Garret and John Herd; one mason, Edward Brinton; one tailor, William Love; one blacksmith, James Read; one barber, Thomas Couper; Nicholas Skot, a drummer; and four boys, named as Samuell Collier, Nathaniel Pecock, James Brumfield, and Richard Mutton.[12]

One hundred and forty-four mariners and adventurers left Blackwall docks to the east of London in December 1606, and four months later, on April 26, Captain Newport ordered the fleet to drop anchor on the southern shore of Chesapeake Bay.[13] The following events were recounted by George Percy, one of the early settlers (with extracts from his account in italics).[14]

Arrival in the New World

The first night, April 26, 1607:

At night, when wee were going aboard, there came the Savages

---

12 From "The Travels and Works of Captain John Smith, President of Virginia and Admiral of New England, 1580–1631," in: Billings, Warren M. (ed.), *The Old Dominion in the Seventeenth Century: A Documentary History of Virginia, 1606–1689* (Chapel Hill, NC, published for Early American History and Culture, Williamsburg, VA, by the University of North Carolina Press, 1975), p. 18.

13 Horn, James. *A Land as God Made It, Jamestown and the Birth of America* (New York Perseus Books, 2005), p. 45.

14 From George Percy's account "Voyage to Virginia and the Colony's First Days," in: Billings, *The Old Dominion*, pp. 22–26.

creeping upon all foure, from the Hills like Beares, with their Bowes in their mouthes, charged us very desperately in the faces, hurt Captaine Gabrriell Archer in both hands, and a saylor in two places of the body very dangerous.

April 27: Some men explored the woods and found a fire. There was no one there so they ate some oysters, which had been left in the fire.

April 28: They explored further, saw a canoe carved out from a whole tree, passed grounds full of flowers, cedar, and cypress trees, and fields of strawberries. They returned to their ship and rowed to a point of land, which they called Point Comfort.

May 13-14: They arrived at Jamestown Island:

The thirteenth day, we came to our seating place [Jamestown] in Paspihas Country, some eight miles from the point of Land, which I made mention before: where our ships do lie so near the shore that they are moored to the Trees in six fathom water. The fourteenth day, we landed all our men, which were set to work about the fortification ....

The Virginia Company had instructed the colonists to establish a settlement on a river so that English ships could have access to the settlement, and to be away from the coast so that it could be defended from any attacks by Spanish ships.

After an exploration of land and rivers, the decision was made to establish the settlement on a peninsula, on the east shore of the James River. Newport, Gosnold, Ratcliffe, and other leaders of the expedition, Edward Maria Wingfield, Captain John Martin, George Kendall, and Captain John Smith, named the settlement Jamestown, in honor of King James. They built a small fort and established a small community. The Virginia Company had given sealed instructions to Captain Newport on managing the colony and a council of seven were authorized to govern. Edward Maria Wingfield, as the gentleman with the highest-ranking status and an investor in the company, was designated as the first president.

June 15:

> *The fifteenth day of June, we had built and finished our Fort which was triangle wise, having three Bulwarkes at every corner like a halfe Moone, and foure or five pieces of Artillerie mounted in them.*

Captain Newport returned to England to bring supplies and more colonists. Soon after his departure the colonists started to die in great numbers, including one of the leaders, Bartholomew Gosnold.

September 4:

> *Our men were destroyed with cruell diseases suddenly, but most part they died of mere famine. There were never Englishmen left in a forreigne Countrey in such miserie as wee were in this new discovered Virginia.*

They were fortunate that the local Native Americans took pity on them and brought fish, bread, and corn.

During 1607, Captain Smith undertook many explorations of the rivers and was captured by Native Americans of the Powhatan Confederacy on the Chickahominy River while searching for food. Taken before the chief, he was later freed.

Newport returned with a fleet called the First Supply, which arrived in Virginia in January 1608. There had been a fire in the settlement, which destroyed the few buildings erected. Stores were lost and the James River had frozen. Newport stayed for three months and once again returned to England, this time taking iron pyrite (fool's gold) for the investors in the Virginia Company. In September 1608 he brought another 70 colonists, who included eight Polish and German experts in such trades as glass-making, soap-making and tar-making, and two women; this was known as the Second Supply.

In June 1607, the Plymouth Company had also arranged an expedition to the North American coast under the leadership of George Popham, nephew of Sir John Popham, a leading member of the Virginia Company of London and Lord Chief Justice of England. The settlement at Sagadahoc, known as the Popham Colony of Maine, only survived for one year. Rice asserts that the two companies, the London Company and the Plymouth Company, had different aims, and states that for the London Company: "At Jamestown the intention was genuinely to settle; cultivation of cash crops was the basis of the colony's economy."[15]

However, the intention of the Plymouth Company was to set up a trading post and to "counteract the increasing French influence in the area."[16] Lack of food, a harsh winter, and poor relations with the Native Americans led the colonists to abandon the settlement. They returned to London in 1608 and the Plymouth Company was dissolved.

In Jamestown, the years of 1607–1608 had been dominated by the difficulties of managing the colony. The leaders had little experience of coping with the challenges presented by the hostile wilderness, men had died in great numbers from disease from the marshy and unhealthy conditions around Jamestown, and there were conflicts with the local Native Americans.

Major disagreements had occurred between the leaders from the very start, on the first voyage, and had led to Captain Smith's imprisonment on the ship, charged with mutiny, but he was saved from hanging by other members. When the sealed box of orders was opened, Smith had been designated to be a member of the council. Conflicts continued with members of the council, with Wingfield being replaced as president by John Ratcliffe.

---

15 Rice, Douglas Walthew, *The Life and Achievements of Sir John Popham, 1531–1607* (Cranbury, Rosemont Publishing and Printing Group, 2005), p.247.
16 Ibid.

In September 1608 Captain John Smith took over the presidency and brought some order to the fledgling colony, with men instructed to build houses. The living conditions were improved for the colonists. He repaired the walls of the fort and the church and storehouse and re-established military discipline. Smith restored friendly relations with the Native Americans, and set up trade with them to gain corn for the colonists; he explored the rivers and Chesapeake Bay and made maps of those rivers and lands.

At Christmas 1608, in Jamestown, the first marriage of the settlement took place, between John Laydon and Anna Burrass, maid of Mrs. Thomas Forrest, who had arrived with ships of the Second Supply.

1609

Smith returned to Jamestown in February with corn, but relations with the local Native Americans had worsened, notes James Horn:

> Nor could he hope any longer for the Indians' help in supplying the colonists with food. Smith understood, just as Wahunsoncock did, the Englishmen's dependence on the Powahatan's provisions. If they sought to destroy the Indians, they would starve.[17]

In the summer of 1609, Smith was injured in a gunpowder incident while sleeping on his boat during another mission to get corn and supplies for the colonists and improve relations with the Powhatan Native Americans. He had made many enemies, who may have been involved in the gunpowder incident, and they attempted to discredit him with a list of charges. He was sent back to England to face these charges, which were later dropped, but he never went back to Virginia.

George Percy became the president and "his presidency is a

---

17 Horn, James. *A Land as God Made It*, p. 127.

chronicle of disasters," in the words of historian Virginia Bernhard.[18] He was president during the winter of 1609 to spring 1610, a period known as the "starving time." The lack of food in the colony was the chief challenge for its survival. The Powhatan Native Americans, who themselves were short of food, laid a siege around Jamestown. A severe drought had affected the region for many years; Bernhard describes the effect on the colonists:

> Inside the fort, people were not only desperately hungry but also literally starving. In a cruel paradox, the more they starved, the less they could digest food. Their stomachs cramped. Their digestive acids dried up. — They grew paler and thinner by the day. — They were listless. They were too tired even to chop firewood, and they were always cold.[19]

Jamestown and its people were in a desperate bid for survival. Some of the ships sent by the Virginia Company as part of a relief fleet had arrived and had added numbers to be fed, but had also brought plague on the ship *Diamond.*

Captain John Smith recounts in his history (relying in places on the reports of others, since he had returned to England), the conditions endured by the colonists during the "starving time":

> … there remained not past sixtie men, women and children, more miserable and poore creatures; and those were preserved for most part, by roots, herbes, acornes, walnuts, berries, now and then, a little fish: they that had startch in these extremities, made no small use of it; yea the vey skinnes of our horses.[20]

The description continued with:

> Nay, so great was our famine, that a Savage we slew and buried,

---

18 Bernhard, Virginia, *A Tale of Two Colonies* (Columbia, SC, University of Missouri Press, 2011), p. 105.
19 Ibid., p. 112.
20 From "The Travels and Works of Captain John Smith," in: Billings, *The Old Dominion*, p. 28.

the poorer sort tooke him up againe and eat him; and so did divers others one another boyled and stewed with roots and herbs: and one amongst the rest did kill his wife, powdered [i.e. salted] her, and had eaten part of her before it was knowne; for which hee was executed, as he well deserved: now whether shee was better roasted, boyled or carbonado'd [i.e. grilled] I know not; but of such a dish of powdered wife I never heard of.[21]

Reports had been brought back by the sea captains returning to England and confirmed that Jamestown and the colony were close to collapse. The members of the Virginia Company of London needed to take action and realized that they would have to send a large relief fleet to rescue the colony from failure, but first, money had to be raised to equip the ships, pay for food and drink, and pay the wages of the seaman and captains. The broad outline of the new plan had been presented to the public in February by Alderman Robert Johnson in a tract entitled *Nova Britannia*, offering "most Excellent Fruites by planting in Virginia."[22]

By the end of the month the adventurers had also completed negotiations for the granting of the second charter and had opened their books for subscriptions to a new joint stock company. Individuals, known as adventurers, could pay £12 10s. for one share in the company stock, but Craven noted that, "… there would be no final dividend, which at that time meant a division of capital as well as earnings thereof, until 1616."[23] This dividend would allow them to have a grant of land in Virginia, as well as a return of the capital with any profit, depending on the success of this new initiative.

The organization became known as the Treasurer and Company of Adventurers and Planters of the City of London, for the first colony in Virginia. A council of men with experience in the social

21 Ibid.
22 Craven, Wesley Frank, *The Virginia Company of London, 1606–1624* (Baltimore, Clearfield, 1957), p. 17.
23 Ibid., p. 17.

and political world took charge and 650 adventurers signed their names to the charter. The Lord Mayor and clergymen led the appeal for funds to finance the expedition and many London companies such as the Mercers, the Merchant-Taylors, the Fishmongers, the Goldsmiths, and others responded and funds were raised. Adventurers also signed up to go to Virginia for their personal experience, which would be counted as one share, at the minimum, in the joint stock.

The scene was set therefore for a fleet of ships to leave England, with more prospective settlers, more supplies and equipment, building materials, cattle, and weapons. In the summary of the *Encyclopedia Virginia:*

> This audacious effort was born out of desperation to save Jamestown, and with it the whole idea of an English Protestant presence in the Americas. Newport, the most experienced mariner of his age was hired to captain the flagship *Sea Venture.* He carried the admiral of the fleet, George Somers; the new governor, Sir Thomas Gates and 150 passengers. Unlike the earlier crossings which transported too many gentlemen, this fleet carried skilled workers: shipwrights, carpenters, fishermen, masons, and farmers capable of building and sustaining a self-sufficient community.[24]

Sir Thomas Gates was a prominent member of the Virginia Company, an investor, and named on its first charter from King James I. He was born in Devon in a small village called Colyford next to Colyton in East Devon where the Bagwell family were well established by the 1550s. His father Robarte Gate had married Margaret Bagwell, daughter of a Davy Bagwell, who may have been connected to Henry's father, David Bagwell of Exeter. In 1585, as a young lieutenant, Gates

---

24 Glover, Lorri, "Sea Venture," *Encylopedia Virginia.* Virginia Foundation for the Humanities. www.encyclopediavirginia.org/Sea_Venture.

had sailed with Sir Francis Drake and had taken part in many battles against the Spanish. He had been with Drake in 1586 when Drake visited the island of Roanoke to take supplies for the colonists. Sir George Somers was an experienced seaman and naval commander, son of a merchant and born in Lyme Regis. He was also an investor in the Virginia Company of London.

Henry Bagwell was a young man of 20 when he joined the passengers of the *Sea Venture* as part of the Third Supply. The voyage of the *Sea Venture* was destined to be one of challenge against the elements of wind, storms, shipwreck, and survival.

Chapter 3

Voyage of the *Sea Venture:*
Storm and Shipwreck

The story of the Sea Venture *is one of history's most remarkable sagas, an almost unbelievable tale of shipwreck, endurance, and human resourcefulness. But it is more than that. The fate of the survivors of* the Sea Venture *reverberates in literature, in political theory—in the very founding of America.*[1]

—Avery Kolb, *American Heritage*

The *Sea Venture* was the flagship of the fleet known as the Third Supply, which had been specially designed to take a large number of emigrants and supplies to the New World to save Jamestown from collapse. The ship had an innovative layout which placed the 24 defensive cannons on the main deck.[2] This provided more space for the passengers, provisions, and equipment. Henry Bagwell was one of those passengers on the *Sea Venture*, with the experienced Captain Christopher Newport, Sir George Somers, Admiral of the Fleet, Sir Thomas Gates, the designated lieutenant-governor, and Sir George Yeardley, the commander of Land Forces. All were members of the Virginia Company of London.

On board with the officials from the company were William Strachey, destined to be the secretary for the council in Virginia, and Sylvester Jourdaine. Both recorded the details of the voyage, the

---

1   Kolb, Avery, "The Tempest," *American Heritage*, Vol. 34, No. 2, April/May 1983.
2   Brazil, Robert Sean, "The Voyage and Wreck of the Sea Venture," 1609 Chronology. http://1609chronology.blogspot.com/2009/06/voyage-and-wreck-of-sea-venture.html.

storm, shipwreck, and early years of England's first permanent colony. Historian Joseph Kelly observes:

> Despite his prejudices, Strachey's narrative remains our most thorough source of the eventful Third Supply—from its departure from England, the hurricane and shipwreck, the months on Bermuda and the events in Jamestown through the first weeks of Baron De La Warr's reign.[3]

Blackwall, a wharf on the River Thames, was the point of departure for the voyage to Plymouth. In 1514 Henry VIII had built a dock here for his flagship, the *Mary Rose*, and it was used as a port for victualling ships as they made their way down the Thames on their voyages across the world.[4]

After the fleet left Plymouth on June 2, 1609, it had to return to Falmouth in Cornwall to wait for a storm to finish and eventually left again on June 8. The Virginia Company had instructed Gates to try the new course to Virginia which was "deemed a straighter, more northerly one than on previous voyages."[5] In May 1608 Captain Samuel Argall had received a commission from the Virginia Company of London to explore a route to Virginia different to the one which the ships *Susan Constant*, *Discovery*, and *Godspeed* had followed in 1606. This route "without fail, headed south to the Canaries, then across the Atlantic to the West Indies before turning to follow the north-setting current of the Gulf Stream to Chesapeake Bay," notes author Kieran Doherty.[6]

There were many young men on the *Sea Venture* seeking new experiences in England's first permanent settlement in the New World.

---

3   Kelly, Joseph, *Marooned: Jamestown, Shipwreck, and a New History of America's Origin* (New York, Bloomsbury, 2018), p. 406.

4   "Old Blackwall," *Survey of London: Poplar, Blackwall and Isle of Dogs*, Vols 43 and 44. Ed. Hermione Hobhouse (London: London County Council, 1994), pp. 548–552. British History Online. www.british-history.ac.uk/survey-london/vols43-4/pp548-552.

5   Doherty, Kieran. *Sea Venture: Shipwreck, Survival, and the Salvation of Jamestown* (New York, St. Martin's Press, 2007), p. 27.

6   Ibid., p. 28.

Horn notes that this fleet carried women and children: "The presence of women and children represented a significant shift in Company policy, which signalled a new expectation that families, rather than single men, would be the basis of self-sustaining, orderly, and stable communities in the colony."[7]

There were hundreds of people to feed on the voyage, including the mariners and officers and the adventurers. Provisions had to be loaded onto the ships, with the *Sea Venture* taking a large proportion due to the size of the ship. Doherty notes that when the *Sea Venture* left the shores of Plymouth she was well equipped with a variety of food: "Huge hogsheads filled with five tons of salt beef were packed into the ship's deep hold, along with casks of salt pork and salt cod."[8] He describes how beer was taken on board for mariners and a better type of alcohol and other spirits for the gentlemen.

Supplying nine ships and 600 people was quite a challenge. There were also barrels of peas and oats, vinegar, cider, and oil. According to Bernhard, the ship carried: "… pots, kettles, dishes, spoons, hoes, hammer, nails, saws, shovels and the like—not to mention muskets, lead shot and gunpowder."[9] At breakfast the passengers would have had "… porridge or ship's biscuit … a staple of shipboard larders, sometimes called hardtack, it was a four-inch square biscuit made of flour, salt and water."[10]

In terms of sleeping arrangements, "The passenger accommodation was tolerable, but far from comfortable. Men, women, and children slept on canvas mattresses filled with straw. For some there may have been shallow, box-like bunks."[11] Conditions on board such a ship as the *Sea Venture* were quite challenging, Bernhard continues:

---

7   Horn, James, *1619: Jamestown and the Forging of American Democracy* (New York, Basic Books, 2018), p.32.

8   Doherty, *Sea Venture*, p. 27.

9   Bernhard, *Tale of Two Colonies*, p. 20.

10   Ibid., p. 22.

11   Ibid., p. 23.

Shipboard hygiene was a bucket of sea-water—for men, the ship's toilet, or "head" was a small enclosure (downward for obvious reasons) at the bow of the vessel. It was always near the waterline, so that the waves could wash through it. Women and children used chamber pots in the below decks spaces.[12]

Henry Bagwell, as a possible relation of Sir Thomas Gates, may have had some advantages and may have been able to acquire a good berth and have his own supply of brandy and wine, notes Doherty:

A few of the "gentlemen adventurers"—men like Strachey who were not just gentlemen but also shareholders in the Virginia Company—were almost certainly housed in the mate's cabin (along with master's mate Ravens) or perhaps in the gunner's room.[13]

Admiral Somers and Sir Thomas Gates would have slept in the great cabin on the high stern of the poop deck. The Virginia Company provided books and maps and other resources for the colonists.

Henry was one of 600—"more than all the men who had been sent to Virginia in the preceding two years."[14] Some of the people on the voyage paid their own passage; others were indentured servants, who signed up to work for three years for the company in return for land. Henry was a member of the Virginia Company, and a William Bagwell, possibly his brother, bought three shares in the company.[15]

The voyage begins

The crew, passengers, and those chosen to lead the expedition must have felt some trepidation not only at the length of the voyage but

---

12 Ibid., p.23.

13 Doherty, *Sea Venture*, p. 29.

14 Craven, *Virginia Company*, p. 15.

15 Kingsbury, Susan Myra (ed.), *The Records of the Virginia Company of London*, Documents 1, 1607–1622, Vol. III (Heritage Books, 2010[1933]), p. 593.

at the state of affairs in Jamestown. On board the *Sea Venture* was a young clergyman, the Reverend Richard Bucke, who offered a prayer for a safe voyage and "Day after day for almost two months, the daytime sky remained clear of storm clouds, the wind moderate and steady, the blue waters of the Atlantic stretching peaceful as far as the eye could see."[16] All the ships were able to keep in "friendly consort together, not a whole watch at any time losing sight of each other."[17]

In his account, William Strachey recorded that, on the morning of July 24, St. James's Day, everything changed:

> Four-and-twenty hours, the storm in a restless tumult had blown so exceedingly as we could not apprehend in our imaginations any possibility of greater violence; yet did we still find it not only more terrible, but more constant fury added to fury, and one storm urging a second more outrageous than the former, whether it so wrought upon our fears or indeed met with new forces … What shall I say? Winds and seas as mad as fury and rage could make them.[18]

The passengers on the *Sea Venture* feared for their lives but they faced another problem: a leak had been discovered. Jourdaine observed:

> … our ship was so shaken, torn, and leaked that she received so much water as covered two tiers of hogshead of ballast; that our men stood up to the middles with buckets, barricos, and kettles to bail out the water and continually pumped for three days without any intermissions; and yet the water seemed to increase than to diminish.[19]

16 Doherty, *Sea Venture*, p. 29.

17 Raine, David F., *Sir George Somers, A Man of his Times* (Bermuda, Pompano Publications, 1994), p. 120.

18 Strachey, William. "A True Reportory of the Wreck and Redemption of Sir Thomas Gates," in *A Voyage to Virginia in 1609, Two Narratives*. Edited by Louis B. Wright (Charlottesville and London, University of Virginia Press, 2nd edition, 2013), pp. 6–7.

19 Jourdaine, Sylvester. "Discovery of the Bermudas," in *A Voyage to Virginia in 1609, Two Narratives*. Edited by Louis B. Wright (Charlottesville and London, University of Virginia Press, 2nd edition, 2013), p. 105.

The *Sea Venture* had been built with long, thick planks laid flush, edge to edge and end to end over oak frames with caulking (oakum) applied between the planks. Doherty gives a good description: "This caulking, called oakum, was typically made using fibres from unravelled rope. Impregnated with tar, these fibres were packed into seams and joints, making the ship watertight."[20] The heavy pounding of the waves had dislodged the oakum and caused the leak.

Gates ordered the men to look for the leaks and divided the men into three groups to pump out the water accumulating in the hold. Every man, including Gates and Somers, took their turn to empty the buckets or operate the pumps.

> The common sort, stripped naked as men in galleys, the easier both to hold out and to shirk from under the salt water which continually leapt in among them, kept their eyes waking and their thoughts and hands working with tired bodies and wasted spirits three days and four nights.[21]

The *Sea Venture* was fitted with three pumps, but the water kept rising and conditions below deck were desperate, says Doherty:

> The deck hatch and the gun ports, the only likely source of fresh air and light for those who were housed in the 'tween-deck area, were battened and lashed closed as the rain began. The normally fetid air below grew even more close and disgusting as passengers vomited almost without ceasing, relieved themselves where they could, and sweat out their fear in the crowded, airless space.[22]

The *Sea Venture* was tossed up and down in the huge waves.

When a leak was discovered pieces of beef were used to stop the flow; the pumps became clogged with sodden biscuits; the *Sea Venture*

---

20 Doherty, *Sea Venture*, p. 40.
21 Strachey, "A True Reportory," p. 10.
22 Doherty, *Sea Venture*, p. 39.

was struggling. A huge wave struck her, and the water poured over the ship and

> … carried the helmsmen from the helm and wrested the whipstaff out of his hand, which so flew from side to side that when he would have seized the same again it so tossed him from starboard to larboard as it was God's mercy it had not split him.[23]

Strachey comments that Sir Thomas Gates, on thinking that the ship was sinking, waded "out of the flood thereof, all his ambition was but to climb up above-hatches to die in *aperto coelo* and in the company of his old friends."[24]

On the night of Thursday July 27, Sir George Somers, Admiral of the Fleet, was on watch and saw a small light in the sky—Spanish sailors called this "St. Elmo's Fire" and it was thought to be a good omen. On Friday the light disappeared; the ship was listing to starboard; rigging, chests, trunks, hogsheads of oil, cider, and cannons were thrown overboard. The rain continued, all on board were exhausted; some of men resorted to a drink, others just sat or slept. At mid-morning, there was a shout from Sir George Somers. He had sighted land and "Captain Newport steered his battered boat towards the complex pattern of reefs which encircled the islands; Somers high on the bow helping to guide and direct him."[25] The men continued to pump water out of the hold; the leadsman put his weight over the keel of the ship; 83 feet, 42 feet and 24 feet were recorded.

The *Sea Venture* came to rest between two coral outcroppings and was held fast. The water crashed through the splintered wood and passengers and sailors clambered to get to deck. Jourdaine observed,

---

23 Strachey, "A True Reportory," p. 11.
24 Ibid.
25 Raine, *Sir George Somers*, p. 121.

"And neither did our ship sink but, fell between two rocks where she was fast lodged and locked for further budging."[26]

The *Sea Venture* was held fast by the reef, but all the passengers and crew had survived. The storm had lessened, and the ship's longboat and skiff could be lowered into the calmer water and all the passengers were rowed to the beach. The crew salvaged what they could: loose rigging, canvas, provisions, clothes, and some hogs who had survived the voyage.

This was Bermuda, known to sailors as the "Isle of Devils." Jourdaine writes:

> Upon the eight-and-twentieth day of July, 1609 (after the extremity of the storm was something qualified), we fell upon the shore of the Bermuda, where after our general, Sir Thomas Gates, Sir George Somers, and Captain Newport had by their provident carefulness landed all their men and so much of the goods and provisions out of the ship as was not utterly spoiled, every man disposed and applied himself to search for and to seek out such relief and sustenance as the country afforded.[27]

The rest of the fleet, which had left Plymouth on June 2, 1609, had limped into Jamestown. Everyone waited for the arrival of the *Sea Venture*, but it was ten months before its battered crew would finally reach their destination, not in the *Sea Venture* but in two small ships, built from its timbers, salvaged from the wreck and the cedar wood of Bermuda, which the survivors, marooned on the island, would name the *Deliverance* and *Patience*.

---

26 Jourdaine, "Discovery of the Bermudas," p. 107.
27 Ibid., p. 109.

Chapter 4

Bermuda: Survival, Mutiny, and Marriage

That first night, July 28, 1609, the white sands of "Gates's Bay" must have glowed with dozens of fires. On them newly caught fish, fat and succulent, roasted in the ashes. This was the castaways' first fresh food since the Sea Venture *had left England eight weeks earlier.*

—Virginia Bernhard, *A Tale of Two Colonies*[1]

One hundred and fifty people and the ship's dog had survived the storm and shipwreck, which had driven the *Sea Venture* onto the coral reefs surrounding the island. The survivors faced many challenges on the island, from mutiny to murder and leadership difficulties, but the provision of food was not one of them. Jourdaine, in his report "Discovery of the Bermudas," commented that they had a good supply of fish, which he described as "very fat and sweet and of that proportion and bigness that three of them will conveniently lade two men: those we called rockfish."[2] Other fish are described in his report, as well as hogs and fowl and all kinds of eggs of different colors and sizes. Also noted were tortoises, "which itself is all very good meat and yieldeth great store of oil."[3]

The men made a shallow boat and they went further out into the sea and caught pilchards, mullets, and many others which the:

---

1   Bernhard, *Tale of Two Colonies*, p. 68.
2   Jourdaine, "Discovery of the Bermudas," p. 110.
3   Ibid., p. 111.

… governor dried and salted, and barreling them up, brought to sea five hundred: for he procured salt to be made with some brine, which happily preserved, and once having the quantity, he kept three or four pots boiling and two or three men attending nothing else.[4]

Sir Thomas Gates instructed the men to make a net with the masts from the ship and trammel (three levels of net) and, with this, caught a huge amount of fish and set the men to work, notes Doherty:

> [By] early August of 1609, the survivors had established their tiny settlement on the beach overlooking Gates Bay. The quarters were described as "cabins" thatched with palmetto fronds. Nearby stood a small enclosure they had built to hold the hogs ferried ashore from the *Sea Venture* wreck.[5]

The island also had a good selection of fruit, including mulberries and pears. Jourdaine described how another source of food was discovered by the survivors: "The head of the palmetto tree is very good meat, either raw or sodden; it yieldeth a head which weitheth about twenty pound and is far better meat than any cabbage."[6]

Attempts were made to get help, and in late August a longboat, manned by Henry Ravens, the master's mate and an experienced seaman, made two attempts to find a way through the reefs. He was successful on the second attempt and promised to return if he survived and reached the colony in Virginia. Sadly, no more was heard of him. By October, Gates and his men started to build a small ship: "the governor-designate of Virginia, worked alongside Frobisher and other labourers, hewing and toting and sawing in the summer heat, providing an example to men."[7] The seamen with Somers continued to hunt and fish, and Somers took a boat and made a map of the island. His men

4   Strachey, "A True Reportory."
5   Doherty, *Sea Venture*, p. 60.
6   Jourdaine, "Discovery of the Bermudas," p. 112.
7   Doherty, *Sea Venture*, p. 75.

did not get involved with Gates and his men. Daily life became one of routine with prayers and everyone was expected to attend.

There was time for two young people to be married; on November 26, Thomas Powell, the cook of Sir George Somers, married Elizabeth Parsons.

> There was born upon the Bermudas, at the time of our being there, two children, the one a man-child, there baptized by the name of Bermudas and a woman-child, baptized by the name of Bermudas, also there was a marriage between two English people upon the island.[8]

There had been no sightings of any ships. The ship being built by Gates' men would not be large enough to take all the survivors. Gates and Somers realized that they needed to build a second ship. Somers demanded help and supplies from Gates, who provided him with two carpenters, some men, and supplies, but offered only a single bolt. There had been disagreements between the two men on who should be the leader of this group of survivors, and Gates, as the proposed lieutenant-governor for Virginia, assumed the right of leadership. Somers took his men, mostly the mariners, to another small island and, according to Bernhard, "He and his men would no longer live in the quarter with Gates and the rest of the company. The two leaders would now have separate commands."[9]

It was at this point that a group of men decided they did not want to work on Gates' pinnace and hatched a plot to escape. A boat was stolen, and they took it to another island, intent on staying there and not going on to Virginia. Gates found out and exiled the men to the island with a few provisions. Soon the men found that they had made a mistake, asked to return and Gates allowed them to rejoin, but more trouble was on its way.

---

8 Jourdaine, "Discovery of the Bermudas," p. 113.
9 Bernhard, *Tale of Two Colonies*, p. 83.

One of the men involved in the island escape, Stephen Hopkins, stirred up a revolt against the leadership of Gates and encouraged many of the castaways to join him. Gates quickly took command and Hopkins was charged with mutiny, but Strachey, Captain Newport, and others secured a pardon.

There was another challenge "in which the life of our governor, with many others were threatened."[10] Some of the mariners set up their own camp, at a place called Bailey's Bay. These men wanted to stay on Bermuda and were also dissatisfied with the leadership of Gates. A plot was discovered that these mariners were planning to storm the storehouse and take the supplies for themselves. "Gates gave orders to double the number of sentinels guarding the storehouse," says Bernhard. "He also doubled the number of men assigned to night watches."[11]

One of the men, Henry Paine, was on the night watch on March 13, and used abusive words about the leadership of Gates to the captain of the watch. This was reported to Gates, who took a very strong action and sentenced Paine to death by hanging:

> After the ladder being ready, after he had made his confession, he earnestly desired being a gentleman, that he might be shot to death, and towards the evening he had his desire, the sun and his life setting together.[12]

The two pinnaces were nearly finished, and the time was approaching when the people would be able to leave the island and finally make their way to Virginia. Many of Somers' men refused to leave, hid in the woods, and would not listen to Somers. Gates sent a letter to Somers and appealed to his sense of honour and explained how their reputations would be damaged if they did not both continue

10 Strachey, "A True Repertory," p. 46.
11 Bernhard, *Tale of Two Colonies*, p. 92.
12 Strachey, "A True Repertory," p. 49.

to Virginia. Additionally, Gates agreed the men would be pardoned, and all but two men agreed to the offer. Says Bernhard:

> At long last, on the morning of May 10, all was in readiness. The eighty-ton *Deliverance* had a 'tween-deck space of four and a half feet, not enough room for an adult to stand upright, with a steerage five feet long and six feet high and a tiny gallery with two windows. The thirty-ton *Patience* had even less room.[13]

They were ready to leave. Sir Thomas Gates built a cross, made from some of the rescued timbers of the *Sea Venture*, and placed it in the garden that Sir George Somers had developed during their stay on the island. He placed a silver coin of twelve pence into the wood and an inscription in Latin and English, which said:

> In memory of our great deliverance, both from the mighty storm and leak, we have set up this to honor of God. It is the spoil of an English ship (of three hundred ton) called the *Sea Venture*, bound with seven ships more (from which the storm divided us) to Virginia, or Nova Britannia, in America. In it were two knights, Sir Thomas Gates, Knight, governor of the English forces and colony there, and Sir George Somers, Knight, admiral of the seas.
>
> Her Captain was Christopher Newport: passengers and mariners she had beside (which all came safe to land) one hundred and fifty. We were forced to run her ashore by reason of her leak under a point that bore southeast from the northern point of the island, which we discovered first the eight-and-twentieth of July, 1609.[14]

The survivors of the *Sea Venture* were finally escaping the island that had been their home for ten months. They had survived many

---

13 Bernhard, *Tale of Two Colonies*, p. 121.
14 Jourdaine, "Discovery of the Bermudas," p. 115.

challenges, including disputes between Gates and Somers, mutiny, deaths, a marriage, and births. They had lived well off the fruits, meat, and fish, and were well nourished. The work on the building of the two pinnaces had been hard but would have added to their well-being. Friendships had been formed that would continue on the next part of their voyage and into the early days in Virginia.

Henry Bagwell would have taken part in all the activities and helped with the building of the pinnace *Deliverance* (see Figure 5.1). He was on the *Deliverance* when she finally left the island on 10 May. The ship was guided out into the main channel, surviving a small collision with a rock.

The eyewitness accounts of Strachey and Jourdaine have provided the detail of the journey, time on the island, and the challenges faced by the survivors; Strachey went on to be the first secretary of the Council of Virginia but returned to London in 1616.

They had no knowledge of how long it would take to get to Virginia, but their expectation was that they would find plenty of food and provisions at Jamestown, so they packed the two pinnaces with just enough food and water to last a short journey. The good management of Sir Thomas Gates provided salt to store fish and they were able to take these on the journey, plus fruit and vegetables. They did not know if the other ships had arrived in Virginia, or the state of affairs for the colonists.

Sir Thomas Gates had been given a set of instructions by the Virginia Company on the management of the colony and it was his responsibility to enforce the rules and regulations, as laid down by the company. He and Somers had had their problems with leadership on the island, but as the designated lieutenant-governor of the colony of Virginia, it would be Gates' role to take charge.

Jourdaine wrote upon leaving Bermuda:

> When all things were made ready and commodiously fitted, the
> wind fair, we set sail and out off from the Bermudas, the tenth
> of May in the year 1610, and arrived at Jamestown in Virginia
> the four-and-twentieth day of the same month, where we found
> some three-score persons living.[15]

On May 21, 1610 they reached the shore within two miles of Point
Comfort.

Henry and all the survivors had arrived.

---

15 Ibid, pp. 114–115.

Part II

THE EARLY DAYS IN VIRGINIA, 1610–1625

Chapter 5

Henry's Arrival in Jamestown and the Early Days of the Colony, 1610–1616

Arrival in Virginia

On the *Deliverance* Henry Bagwell watched the longboat as it made its way across the short stretch of sea to the coast. A small fortification could be seen on the headland and all on board *Deliverance* and *Patience* must have felt some anxiety at the sound of a cannon being fired "when the captain of the fort discharged a warning piece at us."[1]

The seamen in the longboat stopped rowing. The people on the headland were shouting at the men in the boat and the lead seaman shouted back that they had come with Sir Thomas Gates, Sir George Somers, Captain Newport, and more colonists. Ten months had gone by and those on the shore must have been overjoyed that the colonists, sailors, and officers had survived and the lieutenant-governor, nominated by the Virginia Company of London, had finally arrived.

It was May 21, 1610.

The men on the headland at the fortification, known as Fort Algernon, were James Davis, captain of one of the ships from the Third Supply, and Sir Thomas Percy, who had been elected president

---

1   Strachey, "A True Reportory," p. 61.

in the absence of Gates, with 40 men from Jamestown. The small fort had been built as an outpost to guard the entrance to the James River and to watch out for any Spanish ships that might stray into the Chesapeake Bay.

Figure 5.1 The *Deliverance*, a reconstruction of the seventeeth-century ship at Ordnance Island, St. George's, in Bermuda.

Many of those waiting on the *Deliverance* wanted to hear the fate of the other ships and passengers who had left Plymouth in June 1609 in the Third Supply. How many had survived the storm and how many settlers were in Jamestown? All their captains were experienced seamen. There was good news about the ships of the Third Supply and of the survivors of the storm that had wrecked the *Sea Venture*. They had made it to Virginia, but many had died on the voyage. Horn comments on the irony between expectation and reality:

> Instead of a great fleet, pennants flying, making its way proudly up the James River to re-establish the colony, four bedraggled ships, the *Unity*, the *Lion*, *Blessing* and *Falcon*, reached Jamestown on August 11, joined a week later by *Diamond* and *Swallow*.[2]

2 Horn, *A Land as God Made It*, p. 164.

And Raine adds:

> The smallest boat to survive the storm, *Virginia*, was dangerously battered and in desperate need of repair. The *Diamond* had lost its mainstay in the storm and barely managed to limp to safety; her passengers and crew had also to fight an outbreak of diseases on board and most of the men were already dead.[3]

On the *Deliverance* two men waited for news and, with much relief, it was discovered that George Yeardley's wife to be, Temperance Flowerdew, who had been on the *Falcon* had survived, as well as the wife and daughter of a William Peirce on the *Blessing*.[4]

Gates received the dismal news of the poor situation for the men, women, and children, which was "unexpected, uncomfortable and heavy news of a worse condition of our people above at Jamestown."[5] After two days at Fort Algernon, Henry and some of the survivors of the *Sea Venture* had their first view of the James River as Sir Thomas Gates led the way in the *Deliverance* followed by Somers' ship, *Patience*, which carried the other survivors. Henry and other passengers must have felt a deep sense of unease at the realization that instead of finding a thriving community, well stocked with corn and fruit and accommodation, there were many problems ahead for them all, especially for Sir Thomas Gates, who would take command as soon as they landed at Jamestown.

On May 23, Henry had his first experience of the new colony. On landing at Jamestown, Henry and the passengers from the two ships followed Gates as he walked behind Sir Thomas to the church. A bell was rung and the 60 surviving colonists filled the church where the minister, the Reverend Richard Bucke, chaplain for the voyage and survivor of the shipwreck, "made a zealous and sorrowful prayer,

---

3   Raine, *Sir George Somers*, p. 122.
4   McCartney, *Virginia*, p. 546.
5   Strachey, "A True Reportory," p. 62.

finding all things contrary to our expectations, so full of misery and misgovernment."[6]

Henry and the surviving colonists and the new arrivals listened to William Strachey, who read out the commission whereby Gates became the lieutenant-general of the colony. He was given the old patent and council seal; George Percy handed over his commission as president, and Sir Thomas Gates was thus in charge of England's first colony in the New World.

Henry and the survivors of the *Sea Venture* looked at the surroundings and the fort and, as noted by Strachey, they "found the palisades torn down, the ports open, the gates from off the hinges, and empty houses."[7]

Bernhard captures that moment: "An eerie stillness hung over the little fort, as if it were a haunted place. The barracks and storehouse and the church were still standing, but there was no sign of life around them and no sounds within them."[8]

The situation was dire. Gates had expected to find a storehouse full of food and provisions; they had brought supplies from Bermuda but only for the journey and for feeding the men, women, and children from the *Deliverance* and *Patience*. They shared out with the survivors the supplies they had brought with them, which were "salt pork and dried cahow [a sea bird native to Bermuda] and salted rockfish. For starving stomachs unable to tolerate solid food, they made broth," says Bernhard.[9]

Some of the men were sent to search for fish but this was unsuccessful. There were now almost 200 people to feed and care for in the fort. There was a small store of meal which they could make into

6   Ibid., p. 63.
7   Ibid.
8   Bernhard, *Tale of Two Colonies*, p. 124.
9   Ibid., p. 126.

small cakes and "each person could receive two cakes per day and it was estimated that the people could survive on them for fourteen to sixteen days."[10]

The castaways of Bermuda must have regretted leaving the island with its abundance of fish, fruit, and meat. Jamestown did not meet the expectations given out by the Virginia Company in its promotional material of 1608. Gates, in consultation with the other leaders, Somers, Percy, and Captain Newport, decided that there was no future for this colony and they should abandon Jamestown and make their way to Newfoundland, where they could link with other ships and return to England. Henry must have felt some disappointment at hearing this decision, when Gates brought all the people together and spoke to the assembled survivors:

> … he would make ready and transport them all into their native country (accommodating them as best he could); at which there was a general acclamation and shout of joy on both sides, for even our own men began to be disheartened and faint when they saw this misery amongst the others and no less threated unto themselves.[11]

Orders and instructions were published and placed on a post of the church, says Raine:

> With considerable reluctance, the order was given to build caches for storing their weapons and tools; books and personal effects were carefully packed into chests; other items were buried beneath the floor of the buildings. The sailors set about the task of making pitch and tar as caulking for their boats; women set about making bread. The colony of Jamestown would be abandoned, they would return to England.[12]

---

10 Ibid., p. 127.
11 Strachey, "A True Reportory," p. 65."
12 Raine, *Sir George Somers*, p. 125.

Leaving Jamestown

Three ships were prepared for departure and, on June 7, 1610, Jamestown was abandoned. Gates buried the ordnances (guns) before the fort gates and, with the beating of a drum, Henry Bagwell and all the survivors of first colony of Jamestown and Bermuda went on board the ships.

Thomas Gates was the last to leave. Strachey describes when the moment came for everyone to leave, "… when about noon, giving farewell with a peal of small shot, we set sail, and that night with the tide fell down to an island in the river, which our people have called Hog Island."[13]

The decision to leave Jamestown must have been very difficult for Gates as the first lieutenant-general of Virginia. Bernhard sums this up: "The success or failure of England's only colony in the New World, a project that had taken years of work and thousands of pounds sterling to execute, now depended on the judgement of one man."[14]

So Henry left Jamestown and the ships sailed six miles downriver, Raine recounts:

> With considerable mixed feelings, a curdling of relief and defeat, they embarked for England. The sea Captains were again pleased to have the leadership of Sir George Somers and they unashamedly hovered about him, seeking his orders; pleased to be under his command once more. The administrators of the colony just as naturally flocked about Sir Thomas Gates for direction.[15]

Henry travelled on *Deliverance* with Sir Thomas Gates. Captain Somers and his men were on the *Patience* and *Discovery*. All the

---

13 Strachey, "A True Reportory," p. 76.
14 Bernhard, *Tale of Two Colonies*, p. 128.
15 Raine, *Sir George Somers*, p. 125.

people from the abandoned Jamestown Colony were divided among the three ships. They had anchored off Hog Island for the night, and on the morning of June 7 they made their way down the James River to another point, which they named Mulberry Island, after the huge number of red mulberry trees. Here they waited for the tide to change to give them access to Chesapeake Bay and the open seas for their voyage to Newfoundland and then home to England.

On June 5, 1610, unknown to Gates and Somers, three ships had arrived in Chesapeake Bay and anchored off Cape Henry with Thomas West, Lord De La Warr. He was the nominated governor of Virginia and had arrived with 150 new colonists and supplies for the colony.[16] The men guarding Fort Algernon told De La Warr the news of the survival of Gates and Somers, but also informed him of the bad state of affairs in the colony and the recent decision to abandon Jamestown.

While the *Deliverance*, the *Patience*, and *Discovery* were waiting for the tide to turn, a longboat was seen coming up the river: "About an hour it came up, by which, to our no little joys, we had intelligence of the honourable My Lord La Warr's Arrival before Algernon Fort, the sixth of June."[17] A Captain Edward Bruster brought a letter to Gates from De La Warr, which demanded that Gates must return to the colony. One can only imagine the despair for all the people on board the ships, who must have dreamt of escaping the difficult life they had so far endured in the fledgling colony and of a return to life in England with their families and the comfort of their homes.

Henry Bagwell returned to Jamestown and, on June 8, 1610, once again his feet touched the soil of Virginia.

---

16 For more information on governors of Virginia, see *The Hornbook of Virginia History*, "Governors of Virginia." Encyclopedia Virginia. Virginia Foundation for the Humanities. www.encyclopediavirginia.org, January 25, 2018.

17 Strachey, "A True Reportory," p. 77.

Re-establishing the colony

Horn summarizes the abrupt swing of fortune:

> It was a turnaround of heroic proportions. From being on the
> brink of collapse, the colony now had a full complement of
> leaders, some 375 settlers, and for the first time in more than
> a year, it was well provisioned. De La Warr acted quickly to
> establish order and discipline. His first priority was to select
> his council, naming Gates his lieutenant-general (effectively
> deputy-governor), Somers, Newport, Sir Ferdinando Wainman
> (who had accompanied him from England) the master of the
> ordnance, Strachey the colony's secretary and recorder, and Percy
> the captain of the fort.[18]

The Virginia Company had recognized the need for some form of
control over the colonists. Gates had issued "Lawes Divine, Morall
and Martiall" to provide some authority and order, which were
confirmed by the new governor, De La Warr. Henry would have had
to obey a code of behavior, which was accompanied with punishment
for those who disobeyed. "Men were kept busy clearing land, planting
crops, building and repairing the dwellings and other structures within
the enclosed town, or preparing clapboard and soap ash and other
commodities for shipment to England," says Doherty.[19]

Militia were introduced to enforce the laws; these were men with
military experience, who were commanders or officers of groups
of settlers. Punishments included the death sentence for crimes
such as murder, rape, theft from the store, and trading with the
Native Americans; slanders and lies against the company would
lead to whippings; and there were many other punishments for
lesser offences. The leadership of Lord De La Warr and Sir Thomas

---

18 Horn, *A Land as God Made It*, p. 181.
19 Doherty, *Sea Venture*, p. 139.

Gates, as lieutenant-governor, enabled the settlers and mariners to work together to improve the settlement. Horn notes, "Palisades and bulwarks were repaired, and cannons were mounted on the gun platforms and positioned at the gates."[20]

Strachey, now the official secretary of the first Council of Virginia in the colony, has provided a very detailed description of Jamestown in 1610:

> To every side, a proportioned distance from the palisade, is the settled street of houses that run along, so as each line of the angle hath his street. In the midst is a market place, a storehouse, and a corps de garde, as likewise a pretty chapel, though (at this time when we came in) as ruined and unfrequented.[21]

He also gave the description of the first church and the need to repair it:

> But the lord governor and captain general hath given order for the repairing of it, and at this instant many hands are about it. It is the length three score foot, in breadth twenty-four, and shall have a chancel in it of cedar and a communion table of the black walnut and all the pews of cedar with fair broad windows, to shut and open, as the weather shall occasion, of the same wood, a pulpit of the same with a font hewn hollow, like a canoe, with two bells at the west end.[22]

The need for the settlers to attend church was one of the rules set down by the leaders and was strictly followed. Henry and the other colonists were expected to attend two services on Sundays, and each day during the week they were expected to pray at the ringing of the bell at ten in the morning. As an aristocrat, Lord De La Warr maintained his rank which, as Strachey has commented, demonstrated the power of the aristocracy, with its pomp and ritual, in this outpost in Virginia. At the church:

---

20 Horn, *A Land as God Made It*, p. 183.
21 Strachey, "A True Reportory," p. 79.
22 Ibid., p. 80.

> His Lordship hath his seat in the choir, in a green velvet chair with a cloth, with a velvet cushion spread on a table before him on which he kneeleth; and on each side sit the council, captains, and officers, each in their place and when he returneth home again he is waited on to his house in the same manner.[23]

Strachey's accounts provided a vibrant picture of the daily lives and the challenges faced by Henry Bagwell and the first settlers.

The first and most urgent need was for food. At the council meeting of June 13, Sir George Somers, now 56 and considered an old man, offered to return to Bermuda to collect supplies and bring them back to Virginia. On 19 June he left in his ship *Patience*, accompanied by Captain Samuel Argall in the *Discovery* and his nephew Matthew Somers.

During the first two weeks back at Jamestown, men had been sent out to explore the rivers for fish, and the sea between Cape Henry and Cape Charles, but with no success. On July 6, Sir Thomas Gates and some of his men took a boat to explore the James River. One of the longboats belonging to Fort Algernon had broken free and had washed up on the opposite shore. Gates sent one of his men, Humphrey Blunt, to retrieve it, but Blunt was attacked by a group of Native Americans and killed. Instructions by the Virginia Company of London had asked the colonists to attempt friendly relationships with the Native Americans. There had been many skirmishes with them, and Gates had tried to abide by such a ruling, but the brutal killing of Blunt was the trigger for revenge. On July 9, Gates, the soldier, retaliated and led his men to the Native American village of Kecoughtan, which was about four miles from the fort at Old Comfort. The inhabitants were not expecting an attack; they heard a drum and upon investigating were set upon, with the settlers "putting five to the sword, mortally wounding others, and causing the rest to

---

23 Ibid., pp. 80–81.

flee in terror."[24] At the end of the attack, the village and its land were taken by Gates and his soldiers and they built another fort there and named it Fort Charles.

On July 15, Gates left Virginia for England in the *Blessing*. On board was freight of cedar wood, clapboard, black walnut, and iron ore, but also some prisoners, who had been captured in the raid on the village. One of the prisoners was Kainta, son of Chief Wahunsoncock, called Sasenticum. Also on board the *Blessing* was a letter by Strachey with his narrative and eyewitness account of the voyage, shipwreck, and the early days of the colony.

Meanwhile, negotiations were started with the Chief Wahunsoncock. Letters were sent to him in an attempt to establish some peaceful relationship with his tribe. However, on receiving them, the chief's reply was that the English should leave the island or just stay in Jamestown. On August 9, De La Warr launched an attack, led by George Percy, and "wreaked a terrible punishment on the natives of the Tidewater—a punishment that gained the Indians' everlasting hatred," says Doherty.[25] Men, women, and children were killed, including the Queen and her children; their houses were torn down. Many other attacks followed and in one, the English lost many men, including those skilled in mining.

Gates returns to London

Sir Thomas Gates had returned to London in 1611 and was due to come back with supplies and with more skilled colonists to support the growth of the colony. He wanted to share his views on the settlement with members of the Virginia Company of London. Many sea captains had returned from Virginia with stories of the hardship experienced by the first settlers, the difficulties with hostile

---

24 Doherty, *Sea Venture*, p. 142.
25 Ibid., p. 145.

Native Americans, and the lack of order. Gates wanted to reassure the "adventurers" and those people who had invested their money in the company for Virginia.

However, the news of the survival of the people of *Sea Venture*, and the storm, the adventure of Bermuda, and their arrival in Virginia, had been already been brought back to London by Captain John Smith, one of the original members, and leader of the first council in Virginia. At a meeting of the Virginia Company, held at the London home of Sir Thomas Smythe, Sir Thomas Gates spoke to the investors and members of the council. As Horn recounted, he:

> … reinvigorated support for the colony despite the grim news of the suffering of the colonists during the "starving time." Gates emerged as the colony's key witness and advocate, and it was he who eventually manage to persuade the Company to find the necessary funds to dispatch two more expeditions in 1611.[26]

Craven adds: "Certainly it took courage to launch the new campaign for funds to which the adventurers committed themselves in the fall of 1610. The estimated need ran to £30,000." However, he notes, " It is not so remarkable that the adventurers failed to achieve their goal of £30,000 as they actually secured the subscription of approximately £18,000 by the Spring of 1611."[27]

In 1611, there were two more expeditions to Virginia. The first one, with three ships and 300 men, was under the command of Sir Thomas Dale, who had been appointed to be the marshal for the colony, a new position which would give extra support to the governor and deputy-governor. The second expedition was under the control of Sir Thomas Gates with six ships and 300 passengers. It left London in May with cattle, swine, and poultry. Also on board his ship were his two daughters and wife Elizabeth, but sadly Elizabeth died during

26 Horn, *A Land as God Made It*, p. 191.
27 Craven, *Virginia Company*, p. 22.

the voyage. Gates sent his two daughters back to England with Christopher Newport in December.

Governor De La Warr also returned to England as he had become ill in Virginia and went back to England to improve his health. Sir Thomas Dale took charge of affairs in Virginia until Sir Thomas Gates arrived in August 1611 and became the deputy-governor of the colony. De La Warr had died on a voyage back to Virginia and Gates was nominated as governor. He stayed in Virginia for three years and, in 1614, was replaced by Sir Thomas Dale.

As governor (1614–1616), Dale continued with the strict code of behavior that had been initiated by Gates on behalf of the Virginia Company of London. By 1616 he had commissioned a survey of the settlements established in Virginia and the number of settlers living on those settlements. John Rolfe, as secretary of the colony, made the survey and listed six settlements.[28]

He noted that these were: Henrico, on the north side of the James River, with 38 men and boys, 22 farmers, and the rest officers and a few labourers; Bermuda Nether Hundred, the most heavily populated settlement with 119 settlers, men and women; West and Shirley Hundred, located a few miles below Bermuda Hundred, where 25 men were employed in the cultivation of tobacco; and Jamestown Island, with 32 farmers who tended their crops and looked after the company's livestock. The other two areas noted were a settlement at Kecoughtan, on the Hampton River, near the entrance to James River with 20 men, half of whom were farmers, and Dale's Gift, on the Eastern Shore, across the Chesapeake Bay, where 17 men produced salt.[29]

Henry Bagwell first settled on the West and Shirley Plantation.[30] Roles and responsibilities of the settlers had also been noted by Rolfe,

---

28 Horn, *A Land as God Made It*, p. 235.
29 Ibid., p. 236.
30 McCartney, *Virginia*, p. 99.

who divided them into three types of occupation (as summarized by Horn):

> … officers, labourers and farmers. Officers were to keep order and take care of the defences for their settlements; labourers were either employed by the Company for general work and supported by the Company's store or had a particular skill—shoemaker, tanners, tailors, who maintained themselves. The farmers had to work for the Company one month of the year and the rest of the time were expected to support themselves as well as provide two and a half barrels of corn to the general store.[31]

John Rolfe had experimented with growing tobacco from some seeds he had imported from Trinidad[32] and Venezuela as the strain of tobacco, *Nicotiana rustica*, that was grown and smoked by the Native Americans was dark and bitter.[33] He developed a sweet strain of tobacco more suited to the English taste, and by 1614 the crop was being shipped to England in large quantities. This was the beginning of a successful crop which allowed the colony to succeed and thrive and provided an income source for many planters; it also brought money back into the Virginia Company and rewarded their investors, and would prove the salvation of Jamestown and the colony. Tobacco, said Craven, "served not only as the export staple but also as a medium of exchange and the common unit of accounting."[34]

That year, on April 14, Rolfe had married Pocahontas, a daughter of the local Native American leader, Chief Powhatan. She had adopted the English name Rebecca following her baptism.[35] Their marriage brought peace between the settlers and the Native Americans after

---

31 Horn, *A Land as God Made It*, p. 235.
32 Spurling, Rick, "Tobacco: The Intriguing Story of Bermuda and Virginia," www.royalgazette.com/article/20120430/ISLAND/704309994, April 30, 2012.
33 Salmon, Emily Jones and Salmon, John, "Tobacco in Colonial Virginia," *Encyclopedia Virginia*. Virginia Foundation for the Humanities. www.encyclopediavirginia.org, January 29, 2013.
34 Craven, Wesley Frank, *The Colonies in Transition 1660–1713* (New York, Harper and Rowe, 1968), p. 19.
35 Bernhard, *Tale of Two Colonies*, p. 164.

years of bitter disputes and aggression.

In 1616 the Rolfe family voyaged on the *Treasurer* to England with their son, Thomas Rolfe. The Virginia Company "decided their best interests would be best served by bringing Pocahontas to England and displaying her as a symbol of the converted and 'tamed Native American.'"[36] Pocahontas never returned to her father and home in Virginia. She died in March 1617, at Gravesend, Kent, as she waited for her ship to leave England. John Rolfe returned to Virginia and later married later married Jane Pierce, the daughter of another English colonist.

Sir Thomas Dale also returned to England in 1616 and was replaced by the next governor, Samuel Argall (1616–1618), who continued many of the policies initiated by Dale.

36 Charles Rivers Editors, *Jamestown* (Published by charlesriverseditors.com, Harvard and MIT).

Chapter 6

New Settlements, 1616–1625

1616–1617

Samuel Argall was appointed lieutenant-governor in the winter of 1616. The Virginia Company had a new land policy promoted by Sir Edwin Sandys. This allowed the company to "sub-contract the financing of further settlements to private investors."[1] Argall was one of the first colonists to benefit from this new policy and was assigned 2,400 acres for transporting 24 settlers.

On his arrival he found the buildings in Jamestown in a bad state of repair and set about organizing their improvement. His timing was good, as explained by Horn:

> Argall arrived in the colony at an opportune moment. The country was at peace, settlers were producing enough food for their own needs, and the Company was poised to distribute large amounts of land to colonists and investors that would create growing numbers of independent planters and companies.[2]

Argall had a difficult relationship with the officers of the Virginia Company in London. Sir Thomas Smythe, the treasurer of the company, had developed an organization called the Society of

---

1   Horn, *A Land as God Made It*, p. 237.
2   Ibid., p. 238.

Particular Adventurers,[3] which allowed them to control all aspects of trade and supplies from England to Virginia. This led to the settlers facing high prices for necessary goods such as clothes, equipment, and tools, while payment was made from their own supply of tobacco.

An experienced seaman, Argall had been a captain of a ship in the Third Supply in 1609, and had sailed with Sir George Somers on his return visit to Bermuda. He had explored many of the rivers and creeks and had made links with some of the Native Americans and promoted trade with them. His patron was the Earl of Warwick, whose ship the *Treasurer* had taken part in raids against Spanish ships. Argall had provided his men to help with the raids but these privateering activities were not supported by the members of the Virginia Company of London. In fact, Argall was "later charged with neglect of the public interest through too great a concern for his own personal interests."[4]

1618

In 1618 the Virginia Company chose George Yeardley to be governor. By this time, the colony had built upon its success with Rolfe's strain of tobacco and it was able to ship 20,000 pounds of tobacco to London in 1618, which sold for 5s. 3d. per pound, bringing £5,250 for the investors.[5]

George Yeardley was given a set of instructions by the Virginia Company of London in its Great Charter of 1618 by which it sought to not only reform the tenure of land, but change the way the colony was administered. It was to replace the strict rules brought in by Gates and Dale's "Lawes Divine, Morall and Martial." It provided for a more representative resident government, with English common law as the backbone for the maintenance of order.

---

3   Wooley, Benjamin, *Savage Kingdom: The True Story of Jamestown 1607 and the Settlement of America* (New York, Harper Collins, 2007), p. 354.
4   Craven, *Virginia Company*, p. 34.
5   Horn, *A Land as God Made It*, p. 238.

1619, Virginia

By 1619 four corporations had been developed; they were called Kiccowtan (later Elizabeth City), James City, Charles City, and Henrico. According to Horn:

> Each corporation was made up of hundreds of thousands of acres spanning both side of the James River. The handful of wooden towns (there was little brick or stone) that existed in anything more than name were small and rudimentary affairs, typically laid out in a few streets with a church, a couple of storehouses, and several dwelling houses, "built homelike," the whole protected by palisades.[6]

6.1 Jamestown Memorial Church. Courtesy of Jamestown Rediscovery Foundation (Preservation Virginia). Photo by Charles Durfor.

The Virginia Company of London also allocated acres of land for each corporation—3,000 acres for company use, with 1,500 acres designated to support local administration. An additional 3,000 assigned were allocated by the Virginia Company to support the resident governor, known as Governor's Land, near Jamestown. More land was allotted for the building of a university and college,

6   Horn, *1619: Jamestown and the Forging of American Democracy*, pp. 134–135.

intended to provide education for the young local Native American men, and to covert them to a Christian way of life—a key policy for the Virginia Company.

Churches had been built after the first one in Jamestown in 1608, and three more were added, one in each of the corporations. A new church was built in Jamestown by 1618, and several private plantations also built small churches or places of assembly. Horn describes this policy:

> The Christianizing of the landscapes by the construction of churches and places of worship was vitally important to the Company's emphasis on establishing a "reformed" society in which Anglicanism and piety guided the everyday lives of the colonists.[7]

1619, Reforms in the establishment of representative government

Governor Yeardley's instructions from the Virginia Company led him to establish a representative resident government. Two new bodies were formed: a Council of State, with the representatives selected by the company, and a General Assembly, comprising the council as well as two "Burgesses" from every town, "hundred," and plantation.

This political structure reduced the power of the governor, who previously had been appointed for life and who had the option to appoint or replace members of the council at will. The General Assembly was the voice of the people of Virginia, providing a check on the power of the governor and council.[8]

The first meeting of the General Assembly at the Jamestown Church, on July 30, 1619, lasted five days before Yeardley closed

---

7   Horn, *A Land as God Made It*, p. 143.

8   Jamestown Settlement and American Revolution Museum at Yorktown. www.historyisfun.org.

the proceedings due to the July heat and the illness of some of the burgesses. It was due to re-start in March 1620. However, Billings writes:

> In spite of the session's brevity, only five days, the General Assembly had achieved important beginnings. These twenty-seven men (the governor, six councillors, and twenty burgesses) ushered in a new era of colonial government.[9]

There would be changes in the organization of the General Assembly over the next few years, including the Virginia Company losing its charter in 1624, but Billings comments that this meeting "established a precedent for the evolution of representative institutions and self-government in English North America."[10]

The colony needed more people to support its growing economy, as well as simply to replace those who had died. The Virginia Company continued to recruit new colonists, especially those with a trade or skills that could be used to support the tobacco trade. Ships arrived regularly carrying new settlers, including 100 men from Devon who worked in husbandry (which we would call farming).[11]

On the *Bona Nova*, which docked at Jamestown in November 1619, "were 120 settlers, about 100 of whom were 'tenants' (all men) sent to work on Company lands; they would serve seven years, during which they would be allowed to keep half their crop or earnings."[12]

George Yeardley, now knighted, returned to Virginia after a brief voyage to England, and brought back a number of new colonists which included some from Gloucestershire, where his family held lands and manor houses; homeless children from the streets of London, under the care of the Bridewell Royal Hospital; and 90

---

9   Billings, *The Old Dominion*, p. 12.
10 Ibid., p. 13.
11 Horn, *A Land as God Made It*, p. 243.
12 Ibid., p. 243.

young women who might marry the settlers and start families. All these people were destined to live on Yeardley's plantation, which was called the Berkeley Hundred.[13]

1619, Arrival of the first Africans

African men and women had been imprisoned on a Portuguese ship, the *São João Bautista*. This ship was attacked by two English ships, the *White Lion*, and the *Treasurer*, which were owned by Sir Robert Rich, the Earl of Warwick and Samuel Argall. Warwick had led and sponsored many expeditions to look for trade and treasure, with raids against Spanish ships which dominated the seas around the West Indies. Both ships, with their human cargo, had arrived in Virginia in August 1619. This fateful arrival, of course, has been a red-letter date ever since, as the new country tried to reconcile its founding principles of liberty and human rights with the growing system of race-based slavery that was to lead eventually to the Civil War. But such consequences were far in the future, as the small band of settlers — gentlemen, servants, tradesmen, laborers, Africans and even a few Native Americans — struggled to establish a sustainable way of life.

Horn notes:

> By the time the first Africans arrived in Virginia, half a million slaves had already been shipped across the Atlantic to work in Spanish America and Brazil, the majority taken as captives in the vicious wars spawned by the Portuguese in Angola.[14]

The Africans from Angola were seen by the Portuguese traders as good workers for the plantations. They knew how to work metals, including iron and copper, and they were fairly skilled potters. They

---

13 Ibid., p. 244.
14 Horn, *1619: Jamestown and the Forging of American Democracy*, p. 97. Hampton History Museum. https://hampton.gov/3580/The-1619-Landing-Report-FAQs

wove mats and articles of clothing from raffia tissues or palm-cloth. They practiced shifting cultivation and the rotation of different crops and had domesticated several animals.[15]

They, along with indentured servants, were destined to work on the tobacco plantations along with destitute children from London, whose passage was paid by London parishes:

> … the Virginia colony grew and flourished and by March 1620 there were 928 people living within the colonized areas: 892 Europeans, 32 Africans (17 women and 15 men), and four Indians. All the Native Americans were described as being "in ye service of several planters."[16]

1621

Virginia in 1621 had an economy built on the tobacco industry; it also had a representative government and an administrative structure for colonists, who lived on the plantations and settlements and had a voice and vote affecting their lives. More labor and land had been made available, and there was a more peaceful relationship with the Native Americans, who traded with the colonists and visited them in the settlements. Trinkets and tools had been exchanged for corn; the Indians had learned to use the English guns.

All seemed well, but Opechancanough, the new chief after Powhatan died, had watched the English take more and more of his land. A new development to establish a fur trade with another tribe, the Susquehannas, to the north, was seen as a further threat to the dominance and power of Chief Opechancanough. However, he appeared to be a friend of the colonists. The new Governor Wyatt sent him presents; he appeared to be interested in his people

---

15 Breen, T. H. and Innes, Stephen, *"Myne Ground" Race and Freedom on Virginia's Eastern Shore, 1640–1676* (Oxford, Oxford University Press, 2005), p. 71.

16 McCartney, *Virginia*, p. 35.

learning about Christianity but at the same time he was developing alliances with other Native Americans who lived along the James and York rivers.

Opechancanough was in fact planning to get rid of these new incomers, who were taking over his land, settling families, and expanding into new areas, with new settlements and towns. By early March 1622, his plans and successful alliances with the other tribes gave him the power and the men to mount a major attack against the English.

1622, A massacre

In March 1622, on Good Friday morning, Chief Opechancanough launched his attack, with as many as 500 to 600 Powhatan and Pamunkey warriors. Nineteen settlements were attacked. The warriors had visited the area and would have known where the settlers were working, and according to Horn, the co-ordinated attack "left 347 settlers dead—stabbed, bludgeoned or hacked to death."[17]

Richard Pace lived on a plantation on the opposite side to Jamestown. An Indian boy who had converted to Christianity gave his master warning of the attack and refused to take part in the killing. Pace rowed across the river and warned Governor Wyatt who had time to order the defence of Jamestown and managed to alert some of the nearby plantations. Horn commented that: "The attack was a massive and decisive blow designed to sweep the intruders from their lands, a repudiation of English occupation and everything the English stood for."[18]

The Colonial Records of Virginia show the extent of the massacre:

> Here following is set downe a true list of the names of all those that were massacred by the treachery of the Sauages [savages] in Virginia, the 22nd March last.

17 Horn, *A Land as God Made It*, p. 255.
18 Ibid., p. 260.

To the end that their lawfull heyres [heirs] may take speedy order for the inheriting of their lands and estates there. For which the honourable Company of Virginia ready to do them all right and fauou [favour].[19]

The list had 24 settlements. Some were large plantations, some just a house. The devastation was immense, with whole families wiped out, including captains in the militia, soldiers, servants, and boys. The list of the settlements included their distance from James City, and the names of those who had died. These are set down in the Colonial Records:[20]

- Captain Berkeley's Plantation, seated at Falling Creeke, 66 miles from James City: 18 individuals, 3 families, and Joseph Fitch, apothecary to Dr. Pots.

- At Master Thomas Sheffield's Plantation, three miles from Falling Creek: Master Sheffield, Rachel his wife, 8 men, 1 woman, 2 boys.

- At Henrico Island, two miles from Sheffield's Plantation, 5 men died.

- At the College: 17 men died, plus 3 more and a boy at Abraham Pierce's Planation.

- At Charles City, 5 men were killed along with Henry Milward and his family.

- At William Farrar's House, another family were killed, with two of their servants and 4 men.

- Another settlement named was Berkeley Hundred, five miles from Charles City. At "Westouer" (Westover), a mile from Berkeley Hundred, 32 people died, including an Irishman named Francis,

19 Walker, R.F., *Transcriptions from Colonial Records of Virginia*, State Paper Office, Vol. 3, No. 2 (Archives), pp. 61–66.
20 Ibid.

Mr. Dombelowe's man, Daniel, and one old Maid called "blinde Margaret." The other areas named were: Sir George Yeardley's Plantation at Flowerdew Hundred, Powle Brook, Edward Bennet's Plantation, Southampton Hundred, and Martin Brandon's Hundred, where many individuals and families lost their lives.

It was here that a Lieutenant Richard Kean also lost his life. His father and brother arrived in Virginia a few months later. The investors of Martin's Hundred had placed Richard on the Hundred to take care of new arrivals and had sent him a metal worker and four apprentices and a barrel of powder.[21]

In total, 347 individuals died on that day, and Horn notes that: "by nightfall at least a quarter of the settlers were dead and the colony devastated."[22] After the massacre and the huge loss of life, the governor ordered the plantations in the outlying areas to be abandoned and people to be moved closer to Jamestown. The town had good defenses that would keep people safe from further attacks, and had helped those living there to survive the massacre of 1622.

Henry Bagwell's name was not recorded in the list of dead or survivors, and it is probable that he was away from Virginia at the time.

The winter of 1622–1623 was the second "starving time" faced by the colonists. Many attacks continued and at last the brother of Opechancanough offered a peace settlement. A meeting was arranged, but the wine drunk by the Native Americans was poisoned, resulting in many deaths. More attacks against the Indians took place and accumulated into a major battle where the English, protected by their armour and weapons, overcame the Pamunkey Native Americans. This was the "beginning of the end of the Powhatan empire," in Horn's estimation.[23]

---

21 McCartney, *Virginia*, p. 437.
22 Horn, *A Land as God Made It*, p. 260.
23 Ibid., p. 272.

1624–1625, Henry's first patent in Virginia

Henry's patent for 50 acres was confirmed at a meeting of the Virginia Company of London in May 1625 and noted for 50 acres of patented land in the Corporation of Charles City.[24] There had been an instruction to Governor Wyatt from the Virginia Company to make a list of all the titles and estates of land which he sent back to London

The list of plantations and settlements provided an accurate account of spread of the population from the new towns on the mainland of Virginia to many other different locations, including the Eastern Shore, across the Chesapeake Bay.

The land belonging to the Corporation of Charles City spanned both sides of the James River, and Henry Bagwell and another settler called Simon Sturgis were living in a settlement called the West and Shirley Hundred (later known as the Shirley Plantation),[25] one of the named areas within the Corporation, which also included a nearby island.

In 1625 McCartney notes that there were 61 people living there, with at least six males out of the 38 being experienced planters, like Henry, who had arrived in Virginia in 1609–1610.[26] In 1613 Sir Thomas Dale had established three settlements on the north side of the James River, which were known as the New Bermudas. West and Shirley Hundred was one of these settlements. On the death of Sir Thomas in 1640, his widow Lady Elizabeth Dale left her land and property to Richard Hanby, who would marry Henry Bagwell's step-daughter, Mary Chilcott (Buckland) Hanby.

Wyatt's list of May 1625 indicates that individual planters were granted between 30 and 400 acres, with the majority gaining 100 acres.

---

24 Kingsbury, *The Records of the Virginia Company of London*, Documents 2, 1623–1626, Vol. IV, pp. 553–559.
25 McCartney, *Virginia*, p. 99.
26 Ibid., p. 57.

The list included Richard Biggs, who had come to Virginia in 1610 on the *Swan*. In February 1620 he was one of the burgesses who had signed a letter that rebutted the claims of the Virginia Company that all was well in Virginia. By 1625, aged 41, Richard had four servants, three houses, a boat, stored food, and weapons on his 150 acres.[27]

On Wyatt's list for Charles City Corporation were two men, whom McCartney has identified with specific roles in regulating the settlement: William Craddock,[28] who was named as the provost-marshal of Bermuda Hundred was granted 100 acres, and Captain Isaac Maddison, who was put in charge of the West and Shirley Hundred,[29] was granted 250 acres. In addition, 3,000 acres were designated as Company land in an area named as below Shirley Island,[30] and 500 acres claimed at Westover by Captain Francis West.

Martha W. McCartney's *Virginia Immigrants and Adventurers* traces a large number of the colonists, and gives background information and detail of their families and life in Virginia, including servants, apprentices, and the ships and dates on which they came to Virginia. She comments that there were 17 houses on the plantation and the planters had good provisions and livestock and they were well defended but reflects that: "Collectively the early records associated with West and Shirley Hundred reveal that life on the Virginia frontier was stressful and turbulent. The Indians harassed West and Shirley Hundred's inhabitants almost continuously until at least 1627."[31]

Henry may have decided to move to the Eastern Shore where life would be safer, more secure, and where he hoped to gain more land, across the wide Chesapeake Bay.

---

27 Ibid., p. 135.
28 Ibid., p. 229.
29 Ibid., p. 472.
30 Kingsbury, *The Records of the Virginia Company of London*, Documents 2, 1623–1626, Vol. IV, pp. 554.
31 McCartney, *Virginia*, p. 57.

All the individual colonists and families who had arrived in Virginia from 1606 to 1624 came under the care and control of the Virginia Company of London. The following chapter explores the role of this organization, its aims, and the aspirations of those men, from many different levels of society, at the beginning of James I's reign, who supported England's further efforts towards colonization in America. Craven states: "For the Virginia adventure was a public undertaking, its aims to advance the fortunes of England no less than the fortunes of the adventurers themselves."[32]

Henry Bagwell was such an adventurer.

---

32 Craven, *Virginia Company*, p. 3.

Chapter 7

The Rise and Fall of the Virginia Company of London

England's interest in North America was so largely expressed through the agency of the Virginia Company that its story constitutes one of the more significant chapters in the history of the United States and of the British Empire.

—W.F. Craven, *The Virginia Company of London* [1]

Since the establishment of the Virginia Company in 1606, the officers and members of the Virginia Company had controlled the developments within Virginia, England's first permanent colony, on the eastern shore of America. The London-based members were given the rights to explore the area of the coast between the latitudes 34 degrees and 41 degrees north. The membership of the company included members of the aristocracy as well as leading merchants and adventurers, who supported and financed the early voyages in 1606 and 1607 led by Christopher Newport, the latter leading to the founding of Jamestown Colony. Petitions to King James I had led to the first charters, which gave the Virginia Company the authority and right to the exploration. The charter of 1609 provided the backing for a new way of governing Virginia, with its own council and rights to control its own affairs. Sir Thomas Gates, lieutenant-governor, was instrumental in establishing the

---

1   Craven, *Virginia Company*, p. 1.

first council in Virginia, until the arrival of the appointed governor, Lord De La Warr.

The Virginia Company of London, based in London, controlled many aspects of the daily life of the settlers in Virginia and these regulations and orders were confirmed at four Quarter Courts, held in London, where the chief officer (treasurer), other officers of the company, and members (adventurers) would meet and discuss the affairs and management of the colony of Virginia. A preparatory meeting was held on the Monday before each Quarter Court meeting to set the agenda. This smaller meeting involved five members of the council, including the treasurer, and at least 15 members. In addition, a smaller "ordinary" court would meet on a fortnightly basis to discuss issues. As Craven explains, "only a quarter court could elect officers, either of the colony or of the company, enact laws and ordinances, or determine policies governing the distribution of lands in the colony and conduct trade."[2]

1616

Governor Dale had come back to England in 1616, and this was the year in which the investors in Virginia had expected a return for their investment of 1609. As Craven summarizes:

> The contrast between the high hopes of 1609 and the reality of 1616 was all too painful. Six hundred men, women, and children had sailed for Virginia in the first of these years under a plan to live and work together for a seven year period. They would share, each according to his particular skill or aptitude, in the common task of planting a colony, and they would live out of a common store.[3]

There was very bad news for all those involved in the Virginia Company. There had not been any profit, and therefore there were

2   Ibid., p.41.
3   Ibid., p. 31.

no funds to be divided. The company had devised a rescue plan, which promoted their best asset—the land in Virginia. There would be a dividend of land—but only 50 acres per share invested by any of the stockholders. Those planters who had arrived before May 1616 and remained in Virginia for at least three years could apply for a patent. These planters were known as "Ancient Planters"; McCartney explains: "Ancient Planters were eligible for 100 acres of land and had a few other privileges."[4] Henry Bagwell has been recorded as an Ancient Planter.[5]

Growing Independence

The Virginia Company had realized that providing easy access to ownership of land in Virginia could bring a better future for the colony. Therefore, on November 18, 1618, in a fourth charter known as the Great Charter, the Company introduced a new policy, known as the "headright system." This provided an entitlement of 50 acres of land, awarded to someone who paid for his own (or another person's) transport to Virginia.[6]

The charter also gave more freedom to Virginia to trade into and out of the colony, and lessened the control of the Virginia Company of London over the government of the colony. The colonists could hold land, trade independently, and participate in government. In other words, their relations with one another could be as individuals within a society rather than as employees within a corporate setting.[7] They had the opportunity to develop their own communities and build settlements which could be similar to the villages in England, where families lived close to each other among houses, land, and the local church. Craven comments that such towns also developed

4 McCartney, *Virginia*, p. 27.
5 Order of Descendants of Ancient Planters. www.ancientplanters.org.
6 McCartney, *Virginia*, p. 28.
7 Perry, James R., *Formation of a Society on Virginia's Eastern Shore, 1615–1655* (Chapel Hill, NC, University of North Carolina Press, 1990), p. 19.

in New England.[8] By 1618 "the fortunes of Virginia were taking a turn for the better. The adventurers, or some of them at least, found encouragement in continued shipment of tobacco."[9]

Some of the planters were willing to remain in Virginia and two men, Harmar and Argall, who had both served as officials with the Virginia Company, had developed a plan to promote the development of jointly held plantations in Virginia with adventurers based in London. This led to another new land policy to encourage individuals to act more independently with the aim of adding to their colonizing endeavor.[10]

Sir George Yeardley was given the task of developing four towns or boroughs along the James River, where grants of land could be made to individuals and associations. The Virginia Company had enabled Yeardley to establish a representative legislative assembly, so that all those living in Virginia had more control over their own affairs. However, the Virginia Company in London continued to make useful decisions about some aspects of the lives of the colonists and planters of Virginia, as shown in the minutes of the Virginia Company of London, in 1621. These minutes (transcribed in the early twentieth century into a series of four volumes by Susan Myra Kingsbury) provide an insight into the company's control over their lives, and included the agreement on patents of land in Virginia.

The minutes of January 30, 1621 state the "forme of a Patent to such Aduers whose shares exceedinge 50 //acr// are exempted from paying any rent to the Company for the persons they transport."[11] At this meeting were members of the "London Cittizens Adueturors." Their names were recorded as well as the number of shares they bought, and:

8 Craven, *Virginia Company*, p. 36.
9 Ibid., p. 33.
10 Ibid., p. 36.
11 Kingsbury, Susan Myra (ed.), *The Records of the Virginia Company of London*, Documents 1, 1607–1622, Vol. III (Heritage Books, 2010 [1933]), pp. 592–594.

… the Aduenturors aforenamed and such others whose estate are lawfullie come to the said Aduentorors haue not only aduentured and paide into the Treasurie of the said Companie (beside other large Sums of twoe thousand five hundred pounde of olde Aduenture after the rate of twelve pounde ten shilling the share.)

Evidence from the minutes suggests that a Mr. Bagwell attended meetings of the Company in London between January 1621 and July 1622, and also attended the meeting of April 28, 1624.[12] Also recorded was "Of the Sumer Ilande Company vizt" and Mr. Bagwell's name is noted among many other adventurers such as Scott, Farrar, and Mellinge, whose names are later found in the records of the Eastern Shore of Virginia, along with members of the aristocracy and leading members of the Virginia Company of London. If this was Henry, it may mean that he was away at the time of the massacre, and that he made links with several men who became his neighbours on the Eastern Shore.

A Mr. Bagwell also acquired five shares invested in land in Bermuda within the Paget tribe.[13] Bermuda had come under the control of the Virginia Company but, in 1615, a new company had been established called the Somers Isles Company. The island had been surveyed by Richard Norwood and had been divided into areas of land which were called "tribes," named after major adventurers who had invested in the company. There were eight tribes, with the Paget tribe named after William Paget, Fourth Lord Paget. Each tribe was further divided into lots which equated to shares in the company.

At the same meeting the treasurer and members of the company also confirmed the areas of land to be settled in Virginia, and land

---

12 Kingsbury, *The Records of the Virginia Company of London*, The Court Books, 1622–1624, Vol. II, pp. 533–534.

13 From a reproduction map of Bermuda, ca 1622. www.hunimex.com/tree/bermuda.html. Thanks to Bermuda historian Dr George Cook. www.stgeorgesfoundation.org.

identified for public use so that the colonists would have access to religion and education, and:

> ... may have better meanes wherewith all to beare and support publique necessarie charges and other charges for the pformance of pious dueties tendinge to the glorie of god and spirittual benifitt of the people there to inhabite together with the good educacon of the Children and families of this their pticular Plantacon.[14]

For every person who paid for their own transport and charges into Virginia:

> ... if the said pson soe transported continue there three whole yeares or dye in the meane season after he or they are once shipped wth the intent there to inhabit that the said Aduenturors and eurey of them that shall soe at their or his owne charge transport any other shall haue graunted allotted and allowed vnto them or him and their and his heires respectiuely for euery psons so transported fiftie acres of land.[15]

This Quarter Court confirmed the decisions made by the smaller court, which had met on the previous Monday:

> After the reading of the former Quarter Court mr Deputy signified of dieurs Patent wch beinge read in the Preparation Court were well approued of and recommended to this general Court for confirmacon namely.

> A Patent graunted to Sr Geo Yeardley, an Aduenturer who vndertake to transport and plant 300 Persons

Other patents were awarded to:

> Thomas Leusosn for Captain Basse 200 Persons

14 Kingsbury, *The Records of the Virginia Company of London*, Documents 1 1607–1622, Vol. III, p. 595.
15 Ibid.

"To a Captain William Weldon a planter 100 Persons."

"Henry Southey of Rimpton in Somerset, a planter 100 Persons."

"William Caps 100 Persons."[16]

Sir George Yeardley, who had been on the *Sea Venture* with Sir Thomas Gates, was designated as deputy-governor of Virginia from November 1616 to November 1617; and as governor for three years, November 1618 to 1621, and finally from March 4, 1626 to November 13, 1627.[17] He played a leading role in the governance of the colony as well as being a major landowner, with ownership of land at Weyonoke and Flowerdew Hundred. He is recorded in the 1624 Census as living in Jamestown itself with his wife Temperance and their children on seven and half acres, which were part of the 100 acres he had received as an Ancient Planter.[18]

The men named in this patent also went on to play important roles in the early days of the colony. By March 1621 Nathaniel Basse established a plantation called "Basses Choice" and started exporting tobacco.[19] His son, Humphrey, was one of the casualties of the Indian attack in 1622.

Henry Southey (from Rimpton, Somerset) and his wife went to Virginia in 1622 on the *Southampton* with six children and ten servants[20]. By 1625 Henry and five of the children had died, with a daughter, Ann, as the only survivor. Ann married Charles Harmar, the overseer for Lady Dale's lands in Accomac. After Charles' death she married Nathaniel Littleton, one of the Eastern Shore's most prominent citizens.

---

16 Kingsbury, *The Records of the Virginia Company of London*, The Court Books, 1619–1622, Vol. I, pp. 584–585.

17 *The Hornbook of Virginia History,* "Governors of Virginia," *Encylopedia Virginia.* Virginia Foundation for the Humanities. www.encyclopediavirginia.org, Jan 25, 2018.

18 McCartney, *Virginia*, p. 773.

19 Ibid., p. 117.

20 Ibid., p. 655.

William Capps, an Ancient Planter, went to Virginia in the Third Supply with Gates and Somers.[21] In 1622 and 1623 he sent letters to the Virginia Company offering to build guesthouses for new immigrants in return for an ox and horse and men who could fight the Native Americans. In 1628 he was authorized to go to the Eastern Shore to search for suitable places to experiment with making salt by using the heat of the sun.

Law and order in Virginia

At the Quarter Court meeting on March 25, 1623, the "Lawes and Orders" were agreed by the council and Assembly for the running of affairs in the colony.[22] Henry Bagwell, like all the prospective planters, would have had to abide by these rules and regulations. They provide evidence of the strict controls, the emphasis on religion and punishment for those who were found guilty of non-compliance, and the total control of the council in the years prior to the demise of the Virginia Company in 1625.

These rules defined the behaviour expected of these early colonists. Some extracts from a list of 35 instructions:

1. That there shalbe in every Plantatione, wher the people vse to meete for ye worship of God [a house] or Roome sequestered for yt purpose, And not to be for any temporall vse whatsoeuer, and a place [empaled in] sequestered onlye to the buryall of the dead.

2. That whosoeuer shall absent him selfe from devine service any Sounday wthowt an allowable e[xcuse[shall forfeit a pownde of Tobacco, and he yt absenteth himselfe a moneth shall forfect 50 pownde of Tobacco.

3. That there be an vniformitie in our Church as neere as may be, to

---

21 Ibid., p. 186.
22 Kingsbury, *The Records of the Virginia Company of London*, Documents 2, 1623–1626, Vol. IV, pp. 580–585.

the Canons in Englande boyrg in [substance] and Circumstance and that all psonnes yield redie obedience vnto them vnder pain of Censur.

4. That the 22 March be yearly solemnized as hollidaaye, and all other holliday except when they fall two together betwixt the feat of ye annuntiatione of ye blessed Virgine and St. michael Theark[angell] then only the first to be observed by reasone of our necessities.[23]

Other instructions from the Virginia Company:[24]

- The curate: if absent for more than two months in a year, he would forfeit his financial support; if the parishioners were found to have alienated their minister, they would have to pay 500 pounds of tobacco and ask for his forgiveness; any planter found to have disposed of his tobacco before being approved by the minister would pay a forfeit of "double and one man of eury plant to collect his means owt of ye firste and best Tobacco and Corne."

- The governor: he was not able to impose any taxes or impositions unless agreed by the Assembly; and not to demand private individuals from their work on their own land unless agreed by the council.

- For Ancient Planters: those in Virginia before or who came with Sir Thomas Gates on his last visit (1611) were exempted from fighting in any war and any public charges (except church duties).

- For a burgess: no burgess to be arrested during an Assembly, a week before and after.

- The Court: courts should be kept once a month in Charles City and Elizabeth City, for decisions on suits not exceeding one

---

23 Ibid.
24 Ibid.

hundred pounds of tobacco and punishing petty offences; the commanders and others appointed by the commissioners to be the judges with right of appeal to the governor.

- Planters: every private planter's dividend to be surveyed and laid out and recorded by the surveyor; any differences between neighbours to be referred to the governor and council; the surveyor to have 10 pounds of tobacco for every hundred acres; men encouraged to plant corn and take care of it for their families.

- A freeman: to fence in a quarter of an acre of ground, before Whitsun for planting vines, herbs, roots and ten pounds of tobacco and plant mulberry trees.

- Tobacco: on every plantation there should be some men to check the tobacco.

- Houses: every dwelling to have a palisade for defense against the Native Americans.

- Individuals: any person hurt in attacks should be cared for by the company; all men should have sufficient arms; large groups should not go aboard ships together and leave a plantation at risk; people of quality who have not done their duty but found to be ill can be spared corporal punishment at the discretion of the commander or a fine at the monthly court.

- The commander: he should control the use of gunpowder, drinking and entertainment.

By 1624 the Virginia Company was in great trouble; its leaders were in dispute with each other and political factions and leadership problems dominated the meetings; finances were low; there were disputes over the accounts of Sir Thomas Smythe, the first treasurer of the company; the government imposed a duty on all tobacco coming out of Virginia. A commission under Sir William Jones was established to investigate the state of the affairs of the company. This provided evidence of the poor financial situation, the negative impact of the disputes between the various factions, and its failure to support the first colonists with evidence of the high death rate.

In the court of the King's Bench, on 24 May, the Virginia Company's charter was recalled and the colony became a royal colony. A letter was sent by the Privy Council to inform the settlers that their affairs had been taken over by the king. "In general, most settlers, upon being reassured that the king would uphold their land rights, were pleased when Virginia became a crown colony," says McCartney.[25]

An overview of Virginia in 1625

The governor of Virginia, Francis Wyatt, had sent a list to the Virginia Company of London of all the individuals living in the various corporations and settlements in Virginia in 1625. These were identified as Henrico, Charles City, James City, Hogg Island, Archers-Hope, New Mulberry Island, Blunt Point, Elizabeth City and the Eastern Shore. The list provided an accurate account of the settlers and allocation of the land through the patent system and was recorded at the May meeting of the Virginia Company of London.

Henry Bagwell was among the 36 names at Charles City with patents for land from 30 to 400 acres, and Henry was named as having a patent for 50 acres.[26]

Other men named at Charles City were Isaac Chaplin (50 acres), Robert Partin (50), John Carter (40), Richard Biggs (150), Francis Mason (50), and William Bayley (100). Captain Maddison and Robert Bowine had the highest number of acres with 250 planted. Near to Charles City, on the easterly side of Chapoks Creek, were

---

25 McCartney, *Virginia*, p. 13.
26 Henry Bagwell's Patent. Virginia Company of London, Minutes in *Kingsbury, The Records of the Virginia Company of London, Documents 2, 1623–1626, Vol. IV*, p. 553.

500 acres belonging to the treasurer (of the Virginia Company of London), and on the north side, belonging to Southampton Hundred, were 100,000 acres extending from Weyonoke to the mouth of Chickahominy River.

Other settlements named on the list were the Territory of Tappahanna, near James City; Archers-Hope, where the Reverend Richard Bucke had 750 acres; Near Mulberry Island; Warrasquokee Plantation, downwards from Hogg Island, 14 miles by the river-side; Blunt Point, Below Blunt Point; Elizabeth City, where three women were named, two of whom were the wives of the named planters, Elizabeth, wife of Lieutenant Albiano Lupo, and Mary, wife of Thomas Bouldin (the third woman was Elizabeth Dunthorne); the Easterly Side of Southampton River with 3,000 acres of company land and 1,500 acres of common land; and the Southerly Side of the Main River and the Eastern Shore.

An extract from the Minutes of the Virginia Company, June 15, 1625 lists:[27]

> The Eastern Shore
>
> John Blower –140 acres
>
> Certaine others haue planted their no patents haue bine graunted them, The Companys and ye Secretarys Tenante were also seated ther, but no Land ordered to bee laid out for them, as in ye other 4 Corporacons.
>
> Ensigne Salvage Divident [Thomas Savage]
>
> Sir George Yeardley at Hungars 3700 Acres, by ord of Courte
>
> This extracte of all ye titles and estates of land was sent home by Sr ffrancis Wyat (when he returned for England) vnto the

---

27 Ibid., p. 559.

Lds of his Msties Priuy Councell, according vnto their Order in the letter Dated at Salsbury

W. Claibourne, May 1625.

The Eastern Shore, across Chesapeake Bay, was to play an important part in the life of Henry Bagwell. It was where he established a family, played a role in the emerging political and social society, and left his imprint on the early history of Virginia.

Part III

THE EASTERN
SHORE OF VIRGINIA

Chapter 8

The Accomack Plantation and Henry's Early Years on the Eastern Shore

The Indians gave this isolated peninsula the name of "Ye Kingdome Accawmacke" or Accomac which in our language is "land beyond the water"

—Jennings Cropper Wise, *Ye Kingdome of Accawmacke* [1]

The Eastern Shore had been visited by John Smith when he explored Chesapeake Bay back in 1608, by Samuel Argall in 1613 to search for fish for the starving colonists, and in 1618 as part of an exploration to use the salty water to make salt and preserve fish during the governorship of Sir George Yeardley. Salt works had been established, then abandoned, then re-established in 1620. The need for salt led to the founding of the settlement known as Dale's Gift.

Unlike the Native Americans of the Western shore, the Accomack tribes of the Eastern Shore were welcoming to the settlers, aided by the friendship of Thomas Savage, who had lived among them as a boy and could speak their language, and was considered to be a good friend of the local Chief Debedeavon.

Henry had taken his place as a key settler, as recounted by Ames:

---

1   Wise, Jennings Cropper, *Ye Kingdome of Accawmacke or the Eastern Shore of Virginia in the Seventeenth Century* (Clearfield, 1967 [1911]), p. 1.

Among the more prominent settlers of that decade were William Epps and Thomas Graves, the first and second commanders of the "Plantation of Accawamacke," Ensign Thomas Savage, the Indian interpreter, Francis Bolton of the Church of England, the chirugion or surgeon Obedience Robins of Puritan stock, the traders Henry Fleet, Charles Harmar, William Claiborne, and the burgesses John Wilcocks and Henry Bagwell and Edmund Scarburgh.[2]

The family names Epps, Graves, Robins, Clayborne (Claiborne), and Scarburgh have featured in the written histories of the founding of Virginia, from its first settlement in Jamestown to the settlements and plantations on the Eastern Shore of Chesapeake Bay.

By 1620, settlements had been established on the Eastern Shore: Smith's Island; the Golden Quarter (Dale's Gift); Captain William Epps' Plantation; Savages Neck; Sir George Yeardley's Plantation; and Old Plantation Creek. There were also tracts of land established as company land, on behalf of the Virginia Company of London. Other land had been designated for the secretary of the colony, to provide the finances to support that role. Many families moved to the Eastern Shore at this time, to escape from the Western Shore, where a sickness epidemic had spread rapidly through the colony. Hundreds had died, with many settlers worried about further conflicts with the Native Americans after the massacre of 1622.

There was the nucleus of a community, with married couples living on the Eastern Shore, although a census, taken in 1624–1625, had shown that there was a lack of equipment, arms, and provisions. According to Wise, a writer and well-respected historian of the Eastern Shore, whose book on the area was first published in 1911, this census probably "applied only to the settlements and their

2   Ames, Susie. M., *Studies of the Eastern Shore in the Seventeenth Century* (New York, Russell and Russell, 1973), p. 5.

immediate vicinity, and that there were houses as well as people in the upper parts of the peninsula,"[3] Wise provides a exact picture of the people living on the Eastern Shore, and reports that the census states that there were:

> 44 males, 7 females, and 19 houses, 16 storehouses, sheds, and a fort. They had a store with 221 and a half pounds of corn. There were 5 boats including a shallop. For protection there were 150 pounds of powder, 601 pounds of lead and shot, 30 "pieces-fixt" (matchlocks), 1 pistol, 3 swords, 23 complete armours, and 4 coats of mail and head-pieces.[4]

Perry offers this description of the Eastern Shore:

> If the living conditions of this small, compact population were simple, so too were its institutions of government and religion. Captain William Epps, the only government official, provided daily leadership. But the inhabitants had a voice in shaping legislation affecting themselves by the choice of representatives to the Assembly.[5]

These representatives were called burgesses, who could speak on behalf of all the colonists living on the Eastern Shore, at the meetings of the General Assembly in Jamestown.

Henry Bagwell, Burgess

Henry Bagwell was one of the four named burgesses chosen to represent the people living on the Eastern Shore in 1629–1630, along with Captain Thomas Graves, Captain Edmund Scarburgh, and Obedience Robins.[6] In 1631 the representatives were Captain

---

3   Wise, *Ye Kingdome*, p. 39.
4   Ibid., p. 38.
5   Perry, *Formation of a Society*, p. 27.
6   Wise, *Ye Kingdome*, p. 41; Turman, Nora Miller, *The Eastern Shore of Virginia, 1603–1694* (Maryland, Heritage Books, 2007), p. 19.

Scarburgh and John Howe, and it was at the 1631 Assembly that a law was passed which aimed at restricting contact with Native Americans. This was not enforced on the planters of the Eastern Shore but they were advised to be friendly and be careful. People who broke this law could be punished: "a penalty of one month's service upon any free man and twenty stripes upon any servant who should break the law."[7]

Henry served again in 1632 with Captain Thomas Graves, alongside Charles Harmar and John Howe. More laws were passed by the General Assembly. One established regulations on people wishing to leave Virginia; they were required to obtain a licence to leave and had to give a ten-day notice to any shipmaster who might transport them. There were new duties for ministers to keep records of marriages, christenings, and burials, and they were asked to attend the June meetings at Jamestown with the list. Additionally they were required to provide proof of their income and expenditures for the year. All these men were to play important roles in the administration of the Eastern Shore and would become Henry's friends and neighbors.

Henry Bagwell and the Court of Accomack Plantation

Up to 1632, the inhabitants of the Eastern Shore took their issues and concerns on legal matters to the Assembly in James City or Elizabeth City and travelled across Chesapeake Bay. At the September meeting of the General Assembly, an agreement was reached for a monthly court to be established for Accomack.

A monthly court based on the Eastern Shore was good news for the settlers as some of their concerns could be heard at a local level. There were restrictions on what kinds of cases were to be heard, but even so, this was an important development. This proposal received royal

---

7   Wise, *Ye Kingdome*, p. 41.

approval and the court was established at Accomack and empowered to try cases in which the amount involved did not exceed 100 pounds of tobacco or £5 English money, and it could try criminal cases not involving life or limb.

Perry describes this: "As population increased on The Eastern Shore and the rest of Virginia, there developed a need for a more elaborate local administration of justice." The Eastern Shore was seen as a "remote part" of the colony.[8]

The court was organized with a presiding officer (commander) and six commissioners. Obedience Robins was the first commander. Thomas Graves, John Howe, Edmund Scarburgh, Charles Harmar, Captain William Clayborne, and Roger Saunders were the first commissioners.

Henry Bagwell, Clerk of the Court

Henry was the first clerk of Accomack Plantation, 1632 to 1637. He served again from August 1639 to the May court in 1640.[9] He continued in that role after the plantation was made a county. The original name for the Eastern Shore in the seventeenth century was "Ye Kingdome of Accawmacke," and it was later changed to Northampton County. In 1663 the peninsula was divided into two counties, the lower area retaining the name Northampton and the upper area, Accawmack, later Accomack. The two counties were reunited in 1670 to become one again, but shortly afterwards, in 1673, they were permanently divided.[10]

The court records for Accomack-Northampton County date from January 1632, and are the oldest continuous court records of America:

---

8   Perry, *Formation of a Society*, p. 165.

9   Ames, *1632–1640 Acco-N I*, Introduction, p. xvi; Turman, *Eastern Shore*, p. 273.

10 Ames, Susie M., "The Reunion of Two Virginia Counties," *Journal of Southern History*, Vol. 8, No. 4, Nov 1942, pp. 536–648.

"the lives of many generations of Eastern Shoremen are played out on these historic pages."[11]

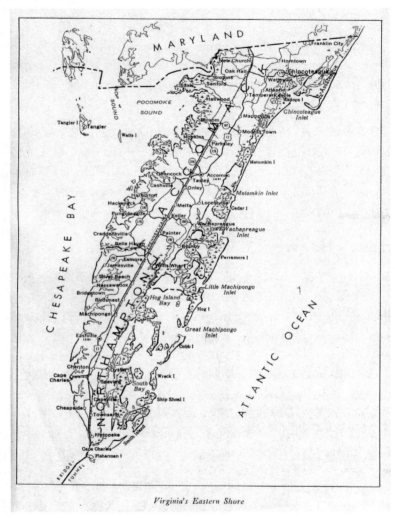

Virginia's Eastern Shore

Figure 8.1 Map of the Eastern Shore, showing Northampton and Accomack counties, and the main town, villages, and creeks in the peninsula. From Whitelaw, Ralph Thomas, *Virginia's Eastern Shore* (Virginia Historical Society, 1951), p. 16. By permission of Virginia Museum of History and Culture.

11 Hickory House, *Exploring the Oldest Continuous Records of America* (Eastville, VA, Hickory House, 2007), Introduction.

Susie Ames, who transcribed and edited the records, provided a description of the role of the clerk. Henry was expected to take an oath to the officials of the court which called for: "true and impartial drawing up of the orders of the court, the keeping of all evidence of causes, the observing of the laws of the court and the commands of the justices and secretary and the charging of only just fees."[12]

Fragments of the first two court sessions have survived. The following is an extract transcribed by Susie Ames:

Order Book, page 1

A court held at Acchawmacke 7th day of January 1632/1633

Present Capt. Thomas Grayes, Capt. Edmund Scarborrow, Mr. Obedience Robins, Mr. John How, Mr. Roger Sanders and Mr. Bagwell.

[it is ordered] by this Court that the now Churhwardens [shall have power] to distrayne up on the goodes and Chattell of [all such of the] inhabitantes of Achawmack that have not paid their duties of Corne and tobacco onto the minister according to [an] Act made by the last Generall Grand Assembly [dated] the 4th of September 1632 And that the [said Church] wardens deteyne the said goodes and Chattels until satisfaction be made according to the tenor [and int] ent of the said Act.[13]

Henry's name is found on another extract in which the named planter, Anthony Willis, first had to recognize the authority of King Charles and was ordered to attend the Quarter Court meeting with the Governor and Council in James City to answer to a suit brought against him by Samuel Weaver. This record was signed by Henry Bagwell.

---

12 Ames, *1632–1640 Acco-N I*, Introduction, p. xxi.

13 Ibid., p. 4.

17th day of September 1633

I, Anthonie Wills, doe acknowledge to owe unto my sovereign; orde kinge Charles, one hundred pounds starlinge, to be levied upon his goods, and Chattles.

I, Thomas Powell, doe acknowledge to owe unto the our soveaigne lord kinge Charles, one underd pounds starlinge, to be levied upon his goods, and Chattles.

The Condition of this recognicence, Is such, that Anthonie Wills doe make his personell appearance at the next Quarter Court holden, at James citty, there to answere to such mattere, as shalbe objected against him before the Governor, and Counsell, at the suite of Samuell weaver, and not depart thence, without licence of the Court, that then this present recognicence shalbe voyde, and of none effect, ore else shall stand and be in full force, power, and virtue.

OBEDIENCE ROBINS
Clericus Consilii de Accawmacke
HENRY BAGWELL[14]

The court records provide a unique view of life and times experienced by Henry and the other settlers on the Eastern Shore, the everyday issues and concerns faced by them as they established themselves in this new pioneer country: decisions on the building of the first vestry, payment for clerks, and the punishment of those who were found guilty of an offense. Another historian of the Eastern Shore, Beverley Fleet, in his Preface to the *Virginia Colonial Abstracts with the Accomack County Records* (1632–37), writing in 1943, described these early records as: "the foundation of our country."[15]

---

14 Ibid.
15 Fleet, Beverley, *Virginia Colonial Abstracts, 1632–1637*, Vol. 1 (Clearfield Company, 2006), Preface.

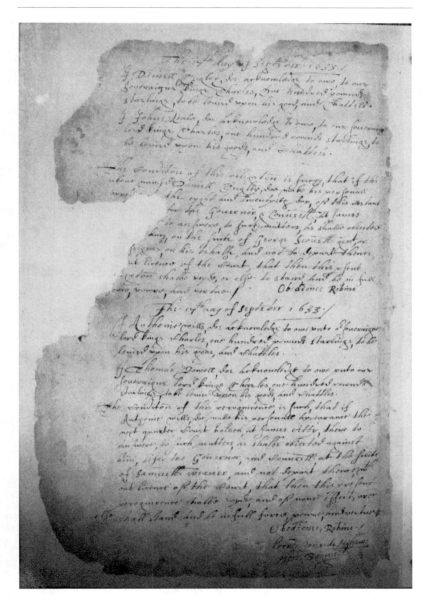

Figure 8.2 Original court record, 1633, showing the signatures of Obedience Robins and Henry Bagwell. From the original held at Northampton County Court: Order Book No. 1, 1633, Courtesy of Northampton County Court, Bayside Transcriptions.

Henry Bagwell is mentioned a number of times in the records, illuminating aspects of his role and his interactions on the Eastern Shore. An entry from 1633 concerning a case with a payment for freight confirms his age: "Henry Bagwell, 43 yeeres sworne in and examined as followeth sayeth, That this depon't py'd unto Mr Sanders 260lb of tobacco or theraouts for the use of fregt't Richard Poopely."[16]

In another extract from the court meetings:

> Henry Bagwell ord to pay Wm Roper 55lb tobo [tobacco], for the use of Capt Richard Stevens, for a pair of shoes for which Peter Hull demanded payment pf the syd Mr. Roper fpr Capt Stevens on the 8th day of January last which debt he was forced to satisfie.[17]

A challenge in court

Henry was named in one dispute with a man called Peter Stafferton, which came before the governor, John Harvey in James City on March 10, 1633:

> To the commander of Acchawmacke to seize property of Henry Bagwell to value of 2,357 lbs tobo according to 2 orders of Court to Peter Stafferton dated March 20 1633
>
> Valuation to be made by a jury of honest men.
>
> Signed *John Harvey*[18]

These honest men were named as Mr. John Howe, Mr. William Stone, Mr. John Wilkins, Edward Drew, William Beby, Edward Stockdell, John Vaughan, Thomas Butler, Hugh Hayes, Vrimstone Foster, Nicholas Gringer, and David Windley.

---

16 Ibid., p. 8.
17 Ibid.
18 Ibid., p. 28.

This order from Governor John Harvey led to an inventory of Henry's assets, providing an interesting and accurate account of those items, including their value, which was expressed in terms of their worth in tobacco, instead of money. Henry's assets appear to have been assessed pending the outcome of the trial. It would seem that Henry was not guilty of the charges and that another man, Stephen Charlton, was later charged and arrested.

Henry's list of assets included two houses and ground, tobacco leaf, and a servant, John Clay, who was one of eight people whose transport costs to Virginia had been paid by Henry. In fact John is the second most expensive item, giving evidence of his value as a servant in Henry's household. The various items, with their value in tobacco were:

22 Barrels of Corne (Maize) of 40lbs of tobacco per barrel	*920*
Bredinge Sowe of 60lbs	*120*
3 Shoats and on pige	*100*
Servant John Clay	*700*
To houses and ground	*400*
1 water Dogg	*100*
Pessell and an ox	*17*
Sum tobacco	*2,357*

All which Peter Stafferton possest of by me
Obedyence Robins Comd'r [19]

The following charges appear to have subsequently remitted as they have been crossed out, but they identify the costs involved in the arrest of an individual brought before a court at this time: for two executions and three orders of court, 50; for two warrants, 40; for the arrest of Stephen Charlton, 29; for an order of Court, 10; for Stafferton's charge at Jamestown, 200.

---

19 Ibid.

There is a record of the meeting at the "Court at Acchawmacke, the 5th of July 1634" with some very important decisions for the community.

> Present were Captain William Claybourne, Esq, Mr. Obedyence Robins, Mr. John Howe, Mr. W'mll Stone, Mr. W'mll Burdett, Mr. W'mll Andrews, Mr. John Wilkins. Mr. W'mll Stone was appointed Sheriff of Acchawmacke for the ensueing year … Capt Wm Claybourne being app Lieu for this Shire did app Robins Gent his deputy[20]

Henry was given the following task: "The clerk of ths Shire also to send Mr. Robins a commission as a Justice of Peace."[21]

Within the minutes of the Court meetings are interesting details of everyday life and decisions made for the welfare of the settlers, which included details of payments to the clerk and churchwardens, as shown by the decisions recorded on May 20, 1636.[22] The order stated that the clerk of this parish should have one peck of corn and 2lb of tobacco for every tythable (taxes).

The status of the clerk of the County Court

Wise observed that, as well as requiring a good education and knowledge of Latin, the office of the clerk was "a highly remunerative position and also one of dignity and importance and much sort after."[23] It was an important role in the emerging society of the Eastern Shore: "the reputation of the early clerks gave a character to the office long after it became elective, and for years the same standard was adhered to."[24]

---

20 Ibid., p. 10.
21 Ibid.
22 Ibid., p. 29.
23 Wise, *Ye Kingdome*, p. 99.
24 Ibid., p. 100.

Henry Bagwell's ability and record keeping is celebrated by the historian Susie Ames, who observes: "one emphasis need be given to him and his work, namely he did keep the record of each court meeting."[25] She adds:

> By Henry Bagwell's faithful performance of his duty, doubtless often a prosaic and tedious task, he set a precedent for his successors in office and also made it possible for future generations to unlock a storehouse of historical and legal material.[26]

Henry's other roles on the Eastern Shore

Henry became an influential member within the community. He was associated with many of the key figures—the commanders of the plantations, the burgesses, and governor of the colony in Jamestown, as well as other important officials and local gentry of the Eastern Shore. In 1636 he became a vestryman at Hungars Creek. In 1639 he became an inspector of tobacco, and he was nominated for the role of sheriff in 1641.[27]

On November 21, 1623, Captain Epps, the first commander of the Accomack Plantation, was issued with orders from the governor and council in Jamestown. These orders were to establish the procedure for the settlers of Accomack to pay part of the minister's salary since the minister, whose salary had previously been paid by the Virginia Company (plus proceeds from the Glebe lands), would now be the responsibility of the settlers. This was agreed and at the time of the harvest the minister was to be paid ten pounds of marketable tobacco and one bushel of corn by every man over the age of sixteen, whether a planter or tradesman.[28] The first minister was Reverend Robert Bolton, who remained for about two years, 1623–1625, and

---

25 Ames, *1632–1640 Acco-N I*, p. xii.
26 Ibid., p. xxiii.
27 Ames, *1640–1645 Acco-N II*, p. 88.
28 Turman, *Eastern Shore*, p. 9.

was followed by Reverend William Cotton, who became the rector for Hungars parish and features many times in the official records.[29]

In February 1624, a new law was agreed by the governor and the Council, where the Accomack Plantation was represented by Captain John Wilcocks and Henry Watkins. This law, according to Turman, stated:

> There shall be in every plantation a house or room which the people use for the worship of God, and not to be for any temporal use whatsoever. And there shall be a place empaled [enclosed by sticks] to be used only for the burial of the dead.[30]

Turman also comments that important officials were to be buried in the chancel of the church which was to be built on the land of the Secretary.[31] Wise comments that the first church was located near the "Fishing Point" at the mouth of Plantation Creek, with a second one built that was "but a rude log structure, more spacious, however than the first."[32] The second church was known as the Magothy Bay Church.

Henry, the vestryman

The church served as a meeting place for the families who lived along the creeks of the Eastern Shore. The vestrymen (churchwardens) were a group of elected officials responsible for overseeing the business of the parish.

In 1635, an agreement had been reached to build a parsonage by the following Christmas on land belonging to the church, the Glebe lands:

---

29 Cann, William R., "Rev. William Cotton," Society of the Descendants of the Colonial Clergy. https://www.colonialclergy.com/rev-william-cotton/
30 Turman, *Eastern Shore*, p. 9.
31 Ibid., p. 10.
32 Wise, *Ye Kingdome*, p. 255.

> The said house shall be 40 feet long and 18 feet wide, and 9 feet
> to the wall plates, and that there should be a chimney at each
> end of the house, and upon each side of the chimney there shall
> be a room, the one for a study, the other for a buttery. Also there
> shall be an entry and two doors, the one to go into the kitchen
> and the other into the chamber.[33]

It was agreed that the churchwardens could be given the authority to
work with the men building the house and that they would provide
the nails. Nails were very important items for the first settlers. They
were used for making the casks (hogsheads) for shipping the tobacco
back to England as well as in shipbuilding and for the houses and
barns erected by the settlers. Ames notes that "Often during the first
decade the colonist, if ready to move elsewhere, burned his house in
order to secure the nails used in the construction."[34]

Henry attended the meeting of the vestry on May 20, 1636,[35]
where a range of issues were discussed which involved the burial of
the settlers on Old Plantation Creek due to "remote living of the
members of this Parish from the church."[36] Decisions were needed
as to whose land could be used for the burials, and land belonging to
William Berriman, William Blower, and Mrs. Graves was identified,
who were asked to inform the minister of the burials on their land
so he could attend.

The clerk was asked to keep a list of the dead and was tasked
with preparing the graves ready for burial. People were asked to give
him notice for burials and would be fined if this was not given; any
complaint that the clerk did not prepare the graves "shall stand the
censure of the vestry."[37]

---

33 Fleet, *Virginia Colonial Abstracts*, Vol. 1, p. 23.
34 Ames, *Studies of the Eastern Shore*, p. 126.
35 Ames, *1632–1640 Acco-N I*, p. 54.
36 Fleet, *Virginia Colonial Abstracts*, Vol. 1, p. 29.
37 Ames, *1632–1640 Acco-N I*, p. 54.

Another issue discussed was the non-attendance of the church-wardens at the meetings of the vestry. This was assessed with payment of 10s. for the first non- attendance, and 20s. for the second. For the third, the Governor and Council at James City would be involved.[38]

The responsibility of vestryman was another source of income for Henry in addition to his role as clerk, but must have been quite a challenge during the early years of the settlement.

Henry, inspector of tobacco

The Accomack Plantation had cultivated tobacco from as early as 1620, and had sent their produce to the Western Shore. A few years later, two stores had opened on the Eastern Shore, one at Old Plantation Creek and one at Kings Creek. The demand from England for tobacco from Virginia was bringing good profits into the colony, more people were coming to live on the Eastern Shore, and more of them wanted to be involved in this lucrative trade.

In 1639 Henry was appointed to inspect the consignments of tobacco and other provisions on the Eastern Shore, which had been divided into four districts. The inspector had to make sure that the tobacco was of a saleable quality. Tobacco notes were certificates that confirmed the sale of an individual's tobacco and were used as a medium of exchange, instead of money. The inspections took place before the tobacco was sent to the warehouses that had been established for storage before shipping out to England. The inspectors were also tasked to make sure that any regulations agreed by the Governor and the General Assembly were carried out. Henry's area was designated as: "from Mr. Littleton's and all on that side: Mr. William Burdett, Henry Bagwell, William Berryman."[39]

---

38 Ibid., p. 55.
39 Wise, *Ye Kingdome*, p. 95.

By 1639 Henry was one of the foremost members of his community. He had played an important role in the administration on the Eastern Shore, as the first clerk of Accomack. Wise states that the office of County Clerk was one that was well paid and the clerk was seen as an important person. He quotes a speech of Judge Waller E. Staples to the Bar Association in 1894:

> … upon no official in the entire county was imposed the performance of more important functions, of whom was required the exercise of so many virtues, or who were more distinguished for the endowments of mind and heart than the Virginia Clerk, then called Clarke.[40]

This was the character of Henry Bagwell. He was 50 years old. He was truly an established Virginian. By 1639 he had married, had stepchildren, and had been granted more land. He had become a planter.

In Chapter 9 we will look at his family life, first as a stepfather to the three children of his wife Alice: Thomas Stratton and Mary and Elizabeth Chilcott. In Chapter 10, we will look at his role as the father of his three children with Alice: John, Rebecca, and Thomas Bagwell.

---

40 Ibid., p. 100.

Chapter 9

Henry's Step-Family on Old Plantation Creek

Henry Bagwell married Alice Stratton before 1636 in Virginia. Alice was the daughter of William and Ann Hawkins (Hookings), and had been widowed twice before she met and married Henry. Her first husband was Benjamin Stratton, son of Thomas Stratton. Thomas Stratton had left a will in 1596 and named a son Benjamin, as well as an elder son, John "heir to the manor, and a younger son Joseph, and several daughters and a wife named Dorothy."[1] They were a wealthy family and owned two manor houses, Kirkton and Thukalton Manor, in the county of Suffolk. John Stratton, as the oldest son of Thomas Stratton, inherited the manors.

Alice and Benjamin had one son, Thomas, christened on March 24, 1624 in Layham Parish Church, Shotely, in Suffolk.[2] Sadly, Benjamin died in 1627 and was buried at the same church. Alice and Benjamin may have made plans to emigrate to Virginia, with his younger brother Joseph. After Benjamin's death, Alice was able to travel there with her son and two servants, John Walthum and John Crowder.[3]

---

1   McCurdy, Mary, "The English Origins and History of Henry Bagwell and Thomas Stratton on the Early Eastern Shore of Virginia," *The Virginia Genealogist*, Vol. 30, No. 1, Jan–Mar 1986, p. 5.

2   McCurdy, "The English Origins," p. 5, note 18; Layham Parish baptismal register, Ipswich and East Suffolk Record Office (ref no. FC 82).

3   McCurdy, "The English Origins," p. 4; Fleet, *Virginia Colonial Abstracts*, Vol. 1, p. 42, Stratton, Harriet Russell, Book of Strattons, Vol. 1 (New York, The Grafton Press, 1908), p. 49.

Benjamin had been left a life annuity of £10 in his father's will and this may have passed on to his widow and helped to pay the cost of travel to Virginia. His younger brother, Joseph, went to America in 1628, became a burgess for the Nutmeg Quarter in Elizabeth City (later Warwick County), and by 1632 represented another area, between Water Creek and Marie's Mount.[4] The oldest son, John, sold the manors in Suffolk and sailed for the Massachusetts Bay Colony with his mother and sisters.[5]

At some point Alice met her second husband, Thomas Chilcott, and had two daughters, Mary and Elizabeth Chilcott. A Thomas Chilcott had arrived in the colony prior to 1635 and was named as a servant of William Stone who may have paid for his passage under the "headright" system. Thomas Chilcott would have worked for Stone for several years. On the list of people sponsored by Stone was his brother Andrew, and three other men, William Hawkinson, Thomas Chilcott, and David Windley. It is possible that William Hawkinson was William Hawkins, father of Alice Hawkins. David Windley became a neighbour of Henry Bagwell.

No record has yet been found of Thomas Chilcott's death.

Alice and Henry's marriage

Henry and Alice were married by 1636, as she attended the Court of Accomack on November 28 as Alice Bagwell and claimed her entitlement of 200 acres of land for herself, her son Thomas, and the two servants with whom she had travelled to Virginia. She then assigned 100 acres to Thomas and 100 acres to her daughter Mary.[6] As the other daughter Elizabeth was not allocated any land, it must be assumed that she was born in Virginia.

---

4   McCartney, *Virginia*, p. 67.
5   McCurdy, "The English Origins," p. 84.
6   Nugent, N. Marion, *Cavaliers and Pioneers, Abstracts of Virginia Land Patents and Grants, 1623–1666*, Vol. 1 (Richmond, VA, Patent Books, 1934), p. 224.

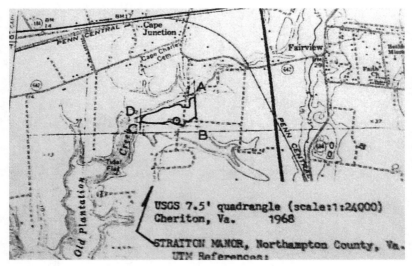

Figure 9.1 Map of Old Plantation Creek. Courtesy of National Register of Historic Places, Inventory, published 1980.

By 1639 Henry had been granted a patent for 400 acres on Old Plantation Creek, next to the 150 acres where his home was located. The allocation of the 400 acres was confirmed at the Court Meeting on July 18:

> Whereas Henry Bagwell hath made it appeare unto this Courte That there is foure hundred acres of Land due and propperly Belonginge unto him the said Bagwell in the right of his transportation of eight severall persons into this Colony whose names are hereunder mentioned It is thereupon thought Fitt and soe ordered that the same bee hereby accordingely certified unto the Governor and Counsell at James Citty at the request of him the said Bagwell For the obteyninge of a Patente for the Enjoyeinge of the said land due unto him.
>
> Names given as: William Whitehart, Andrew Bashawe, Michael Williams, John Cley, Thomas Evans, William Powell, Richard Smith, Mary Vaughan.[7]

---

7   Ames, *1632–1640 Acco-N I*, Introduction, p. 148.

Henry's patent for the 400 acres of land was confirmed in the official papers, held in the Archives of the Library of Virginia:

Location: Accomack County

Description: 400 acres butting on the old plantaceon Creek west northerly being a neck of land bounded on the So. side with a creeke called Johnny Boyes Branch.[8]

Another reference to Henry's land is recorded in Fleet's Abstracts:

William Berriman petitions for 250 acres on Old Plantation Creek, adjacent to the land of Henry Carslys (Carsley) called by the name of Fishing Point Neck and adjacent SW on the creek that parts Henry Bagwell's land and the said Creek.[9]

Life on Old Plantation Creek

Colonists had started building homesteads on small tracts of land on both sides of the creek and these were seen as being in remote locations.[10] Billings described the evolution from the temporary houses of the settlers to a more permanent frame-built house:

The settler first sought to erect a temporary shelter against the elements, so his initial home was likely to be one-room, thatched roof that the Englishmen called a cottage. Constructed of wattle and daub, the cottages often lacked windows and wooden flooring, although sometimes included a small attic.

They were heated by and lit by fireplaces made of logs chinked and plastered with clay ... Customarily frame houses were single bay, story-and-a half construction.

To save space, outside chimneys, either catted or brick were

---

8   Library of Virginia Archives, Land Office patent no. 1, 1623–1643 (v.1 and 2), p. 664 (reel 1).
9   Fleet, *Virginia Colonial Abstracts*, Vol. 1, p. 18.
10 McCartney, *Virginia*, p.72.

located at either end of the building, and instead of thatching, builders roofed these homes with wooden shingles [tiles made of wood].[11]

Henry and Alice may have lived in such a house with Thomas, Mary, and Elizabeth. As their family expanded they would have added rooms.

The Bagwell family may have been able to afford furniture brought on the ships from England; otherwise, tables were made from planks of wood, and stools and chairs made from the local wood, also used to make the wooden plates for their food. A planter was expected to keep sheep, pigs, and cattle, which would be marked with the owner's special mark and registered at the County Court. They grew their own corn and wheat and tobacco as described by Ames: "In addition to the fields of tobacco, grain and vegetables, each planter had a meadow, a wasteland and woodland, an important part of the estate from the point of view of the livestock industry."[12]

The colonists relied on pathways to reach each other, and bridges were built over some of the creeks. There were few horses in on the Eastern Shore at this time. Perry notes that "… the condition of the roads in this frontier society and, more importantly, the geographic fragmentation caused by the numerous waterways hindered the use of horses."[13]

The other way to travel was by water. Ownership of a boat for the early colonist was essential for trading and moving around the waterways of the Eastern Shore, and socializing with other families.

One of Henry's neighbours was Daniel Cugley, who died in 1641. The inventory of his estate not only provides an interesting account

---

11 Billings, *The Old Dominion*, p. 290.

12 Ames, *Studies of the Eastern Shore*, p. 55.

13 Perry, *Formation of a Society*, p. 46.

of his assets, furniture, and ownership of animals, but the sale of his ship, which was bought by another neighbor, Alexander Mountney, for 525 pounds of tobacco. Also included with the vessel were the rigging, two cables, two anchors, ropes, and an old sail. The sale of Daniel's goods was held at "outcry" (auction) on the last day of May 1641. The detail of the items in the inventory are each given a relative value in terms of tobacco. There were 33 lots to be auctioned, including a feather bed, bolster rug, and curtains valued at 400 pounds of tobacco; five pewter dishes at 150; an iron pot, 129; and a pistol at 67.

Henry attended the auction and paid for "three Mattes and a Chafing dish and candlestick for the sum of 35 pounds of tobacco." Also valued at 300 pounds were 14 hogs big and small.

Henry and Alice's first family

Henry and Alice were an established couple on Old Plantation Creek and their first family grew up in a secure society with laws established by the County Court, which sorted out disputes of neighbors and minor offences and controlled many aspects of their lives. The vestry was a vital part of the community, part of the county government, and a place for social gatherings for the residents as well as the center for religion.

The noted historian for the Eastern Shore, Susie Ames, transcribed the original court records of Accomack-Northampton in two volumes, 1632–1640 and 1640–1645. Within these records are the stories of the early pioneer families of the Eastern Shore, their challenges, family life, ownership of land, property, and plantations. Wills and inventories have survived, providing evidence of the realities for young people growing up, their marriages, and challenges of surviving in the pioneer frontier of the Eastern Shore.

Thomas Stratton's story

Thomas Stratton was about 12 when his mother married Henry. She had attended the court in 1636 to claim land on behalf of herself and Thomas. In 1643 he was 19 years of age and accused of taking a boat from a neighbor, Thomas Hunt. The boat had been damaged in a storm and split. On February 10, the court decided: "Arbitration enjoyned to satisfy and pay unto the said Thomas Hunt Fower hundreds pounds of Merchantable tobacco with such charges bee expended in the suite."[14]

Alice Bagwell came back to the court in April 1643 to support her son: "It is ordered upon the Affadavit of Alice Bagwell That Thomas Stratton shall be cleared and Free from any service Claymed by Thomas Hunt. And that Thomas Hunt shall pay Court Charges." Further support from a family member was also noted: a John Stratton went to visit the damaged boat with some of the arbitrators and confirmed he would provide payment due to Hunt, as Thomas was under 21.[15] This may be the John Stratton who went to the Massachuetts Bay Colony with his mother and sisters.

In 1654, at the age of 30, Thomas acquired more land in his own name: 107 acres for the transportation of Alice Stratton and Thomas with an assignment of 150 acres.[16] In 1656 he married a widow, Agnes Barnes, and they set up their own homestead and started a family. Ann was born in 1656 and Benjamin on February 25, 1657.[17]

Thomas died in 1659 at the age of 35 and in his will, proved on November 2, he left bequests to Agnes, his daughter Ann and son Benjamin, his "sister Hanby," and his brothers John and Thomas Bagwell.[18] This "sister Hanby" is his half-sister, Mary Chilcott. John

14 Ames, *1640–1645 Acco-N II*, p. 328.

15 Ibid., p.283.

16 Nugent, *Cavaliers and Pioneers*, Vol. 1, p. 293.

17 McCurdy, "The English Origins," p. 15.

18 Ibid., p. 12, n. 64.

and Thomas Bagwell were his half-brothers, the sons born to Alice and Henry after their marriage in 1636.

Mary Chilcott's story: Marriage and divorce

Mary was married twice, first to Richard Buckland, and secondly to Richard Hanby (Hamby). Her first husband brought many difficulties to their marriage and his bad behavior resulted in one of the few recorded divorces in the early days of the settlement. Henry helped Mary and her first husband Richard Buckland with a gift of cattle and building a house, which were recorded in the minutes in the court records of 1645:[19]

> These present witness That I Henry Bagwell doe by these presents give unto Mary Buckland one Cowe with her increase and heifer which is amongst the Cattle of Mrs. Littleton provided the sayde Bagwell hath the first Cowe Calfe that either the said Cowe of heifer bringeth. And the said Richard shall not have the power to dispose of them or their increase male nor Female unless it appear to be to their releife as buying cloathes but not to dispose of any breeders but they remayne For the use of the said Mary and hir children to which I put my hand this thirteenth day of November 1644 And this I promise to record in the courte Booke witness my hand in the presence of
>
> *Henry Bagwell*

There is also a sequence of references in the minutes in the court records in connection with Henry's help with a house. There is a description of the proposed house, problems with the builders, detail of the payment for the building, and the involvement of assessors to provide witness statements.

---

19 Ames, *1640–1645 Acco-N II*, p. 438.

A deposition from Richard was recorded:

January 7 1644

This deponent sayth That Mathew Pett deceased was by agreement under his hand to build this deponent a house of Twenty Foote longe with a welch Chimney in it besides and fifteen Foote Broade with a partition and buttery. And this deponent gave the said Pett in full satisfaction for the said work Two hundred and Forty pounds of Tobacco and an Ewe Kidd.

Richard Buckland[20]

Henry went to the open court which indicated he had paid for the house for the use of Richard Buckland.

April 29, 1645

[It is ordered by this Court] That Thomas Hunt and John Dennis shall View what is wanting to finishing of a house which Mathew Pett deceased was by agreement to build for Richard Buckland having Received payment (Viz) of Fowere lengths of Boards and a partition and a Weltch Chimney at the end of the house, and to make Report therof at the next County Court houlden at Northampton.

Witnessed by *Edwyn Conaway Clericus*[21]

Two assessors were appointed to visit the house and report back to the court. This was undertaken by Thomas Hunt and John Dennis:

… our opinion is that the worke that is to be doe about finishing of the house is worth Two hundred and Twenty Five pounds of Tobacco being to doe one half of the weatherboard partition weltch chimney and loft to laye and dore.[22]

20 Ibid., p. 395.
21 Ibid., p. 425-427.
22 Ibid., p. 436.

Richard had more trouble in 1644: he owed money to another settler, was charged 30 pounds of tobacco for profaning the word of God, and given another fine of 20 pounds for unjust molestation.[23]

He had been punished in 1646 and 1648 for his immoral relationship with another settler called Mary Russell who had given birth to his son. His wife Mary petitioned for divorce in 1655, and on 30 August the court ordered him to be whipped and banished from the county of Northampton, and granted Mary a divorce.[24] She was free to remarry and by 1656 had married Richard Hanby. This marriage provided her with security, wealth, property, and land. Born in Westminster in 1626, Richard Hanby had been named in the 1641 will of Lady Dale, the widow of Sir Thomas Dale, who was governor of Virginia in 1611 and 1614–1616. Richard and his father William were both named in the will as executors along with a William Shrimpton. William Hanby had been an overseer of Lady's Dale land in Virginia.[25]

Richard and Mary Hanby had two children, Elizabeth and Rebecca.

Elizabeth Chilcott's story: The frontier woman

The date of Elizabeth's birth has not yet been found but at some point she married Tobias Selve (Selby). He came to Virginia under the "headright" system and was noted in the records of the court in September 1641 as one of the men transported by William Andrews.[26] It was noted in the court records that Tobias was owed 300 pecks of corn from another settler, John Holloway. He was witness to another estate in 1644.

In 1644 there had been another attack on the colonists, by the tribes on the Western Shore, in which more than 400 settlers had

---

23 Ibid., p. 376.
24 Perry, *Formation of a Society*, p. 234.
25 McCartney, *Virginia*, p. 358.
26 Ames, *1640–1645 Acco-N II*, p. 116.

been killed. The tribes of the Eastern Shore had been encouraged to rise against the English, but they had refused to do so as they had developed a good relationship with the settlers.

In October 1650, military districts were again established with local commanders, and Colonel Edmund Scarburgh was appointed for Occahannock Creek. He was a member of the gentry who had exploited his position and had been brought before the County Court for many incidents. These included selling guns to the Native Americans, which had been banned by the Assembly. In 1651 there was talk of a conspiracy in which some members of the local tribes on the Eastern Shore were thought to be planning to attack the settlers.

On hearing of a potential conspiracy, Edmund Scarburgh encouraged others to mount an attack on the local tribes, and they left Occahannock Creek on April 29 with the aim "to capture or kill the King of Pocomoke, the leading spirit of the supposed conspiracy."[27] In the words of Wise:

> It was not long before the formidable mounted band fell upon the natives, whom they shot at, and slashed with their sabres and long hunting knives. Capturing a number of amazed natives, Scarburgh ordered their bows to be cut and that the two of them he believed to be ringleaders be bound neck and heels with a chain.[28]

Elizabeth Selve was involved in another incident where she had shot at an Indian. Such attacks were not supported by the governor, William Berkeley, or the Council in James City. William Andrews was asked to placate the Pocomoke tribe with gifts, and he sent 100 lengths of roanoke. These were polished shells, rubbed by hand and formed into beads, and used as money by the Native Americans. Willard describes the beads as of different value according to their color, with black or purple being worth twice as much as white beads.

---

27 Wise, *Ye Kingdome*, pp. 117–118.
28 Ibid., p. 119.

The beads could be strung together into belts measured in terms of length of an arm from the fingertip to the elbow.[29] Governor Berkeley also sent ten weeding hoes to the King of Metomkin, and the two Indians who had been chained were to receive 20 arms' lengths of roanoke. Wise confirms that even the Indian shot by Elizabeth would receive compensation: "… to the Indian shot by the wife of Toby Selve, 20 arms' length of roanoke."[30] However, he comments that the reason she may have shot an Indian was because he was trying to steal items from their homestead, rather than as part of an organized attack.

Scarburgh and Thomas Johnson went for trial at James City but were not charged as they provided evidence that there had been a real concern for the safety of the settlers.

These incidents led to a court order in the July court for the planters to take measures to protect themselves and be prepared for attacks. In the words of Wise, this order instructed that:

> … twenty-five horses and mares, with saddles and bridles, were to be provided by the planters; and if enough volunteers did not appear, men were to be pressed into the service by the sheriff on the following afternoon at three o'clock at the house of Richard Bayly, of Nuswattocks. Each man was to bring with him half a pound of powder, with shot and bullet and rations for a week, and was to be armed with pistols, carbine and short sword.[31]

However, relations with the Native American tribes improved, and the court gave orders that provided compensation for any land taken by an English settler. The King of Metomkin followed with punishment for any of his own men who had been found guilty of stealing

---

29 Willard, Fred, "Trade Items as Transfer of Money." Accessed via
    https://www.lost-colony.com/trade.html.
30 Wise, *Ye Kingdome*, p. 119.
31 Ibid., p. 121.

from the planters. In April 1654, he provided the settlers with one hundred lengths of roanoke as some of the young men of the tribe had been found guilty of killing their hogs.[32] Perhaps with peaceful relations established, the Selve family were then able to relax and enjoy their homestead in this wild frontier world on the fringes of the Eastern Shore.

In 1657 Elizabeth received two gifts, one deeded to her by her half-sister, Rebecca (Bagwell) Fisher, who also deeded a gift of a calf-cow to Elizabeth's older daughter, Rebecca. If Elizabeth's daughter Rebecca died, the calf-cow and any increase were to be deeded to her second daughter, Elizabeth. Another daughter, Clemency, received a gift of a cow from a Tomas Parker. Tobias and Elizabeth also had a fourth daughter, Matilda.

Ann and William Hawkins' story

Alice's parents had also emigrated to the Eastern Shore and lived near to Henry and Alice on Old Plantation Creek. Perry noted in *Formation of a Society on Virginia's Eastern Shore* that "Relatives generally lived near one another and, as all landholders who lived close together, exchanged visits, favors, and support."[33] Also noted was that "Hookings, Smith, and Stratton all lived near one another on Plantation Creek."[34]

Ann and William Hawkins did not patent any land and probably lived in a house on the Bagwell or Stratton lands.

In 1646, Henry was named as an appraiser for the estate of his father-in-law, William, and in the same year was named as an executor of the will of his mother-in-law, Ann. Like the inventories and wills of Thomas and William Chappell of Exeter in the 1580s, the

---

32 Ibid., p. 122.
33 Perry, *Formation of a Society*, p. 94.
34 Ibid., p. 94.

inventories of the early Virginian planters have provided a useful record of the possessions of the settler in the 1640s, as described by Billings:

> Certain household items were highly prized for their usefulness and were therefore passed onto one generation of a family to another. Usually these items were not readily available in Virginia or were beyond the colonists to make for themselves. Weapons, cast-iron pots, tools, and flocked mattresses were commonly willed to a favorite child or relative.[35]

William Hookings was mentioned in the minutes of Northampton Court on several occasions, and one such mention revealed the importance of the ownership of a gun and a shirt:

February 10, 1644

> The resolution — Whereas it appeareth unto this Court by sufficient testimony That Francis Posey absolutlely sold a gunn that hee left in the Custody of William Johnson unto William Hookings hee the said Hookings satisfying that the said Johnson for a Course shirt which the said Posie bought of the said Johnson. It is therefore ordered by this Court That the said Johnson shall forthwith deliver the said Hookings or his Assignee the said gunn And the said Hookings shall make payment for the sayde Course Shirt.[36]

A court record for William Hookings confirmed a voyage from Maryland with a John Robinson, who owed money to Hookings for payment for the voyage. Robinson had hired an attorney, William Johnson, to represent him, and was the subject for two more notices to the court. The dealings of individual settlers were brought before the courts and were solved with payment of a defined amount of tobacco;

---

35 Billings, *The Old Dominion*, p. 294.
36 Ames, *1640–1645 Acco-N II*, p. 328.

in this case the court agreed that Hookings should receive the "debt of 362 pounds of tobacco being two hundred thirty and two pounds of tobacco unto the said William Hookings."[37]

Ann died in 1646, and her will was probated on 11 November of the same year.[38] She left one of the runlett's (a small barrel which could hold fourteen pounds of tobacco) to Thomas Stratton (her grandson), a frying pan, and kettle. She also left her plantation for four years with Richard Symth; this may be the Richard Smith who was named on the list of people under the "headright" of Henry Bagwell in 1639.

Ann left other bequests:

Francis Harvey — debt that Mr Scarburgh owed

Elizabeth West and John Russell — each has one cowcalf

Goodman Harlowe — two barrels of corne

Charles Russell — a Carpet

Margery Williams, wife of Henry — my stuffe gowne

Mary Buckland — quiofe, a cross cloth, an apron, and handkerchief

Kinsman William Gower — shaote (with John Damdys) [young hog]

To John and Thomas Bagwell [her grandsons, with no allocation]

To Rebecca Bagwell — one stuffe petticoat [her granddaughter]

To John Dandy — 2 bushels of meale (in the hands of Mr Roberts)

Great iron kettle — which was payed out of the estate of William Hawkins

---

37 Ibid., p. 329.
38 Miles, Barry and Miles, M.K., *Miles Files*, Virginia Eastern Shore Library, Accomack. http://espl-genealogy.org/MilesFiles/site/index.htm; Perry, *Formation of a Society*, p. 94, note 10.

The executor of her will was her son-in-law, Henry Bagwell, and the witnesses were a John Danby and her grandson, Thomas Stratton.

On her death bed, she left instructions for a 16 gallon kettle to be returned to the owner, John Danby.[39] The remainder of the estate was left to her daughter, Alice Bagwell; furniture went to her grandson, John Bagwell; and a pot hanger to the other grandson, Thomas Bagwell.

39 Perry, *Formation of a Society*, p. 560.

Chapter 10

Henry and Alice Bagwell's Family: Births, Deaths, and Family Life

Henry and Alice's first son, John, was born in about 1640, and this is confirmed in a deposition of March 22, 1665/6 where his age was given as 25. Two more children were born: Rebecca, in about 1641, and Thomas in about 1642. By this time Henry was in his early fifties and Alice was around 38. Alice's parents, William and Ann Hawkins lived close by and would have been able to help Alice with her young family. Sadly they both died in 1646.

John Bagwell's story, and the death of Henry's first grandson

In 1663, at the age of about 23, John deeded 200 acres of his father Henry's original patent of 400 acres in Accomack to his brother Thomas, and in 1672, on March 25, he had a patent for 600 acres at the head of Great Metomkin Creek in Accomack County.[1]

John married Ann (her surname has not yet been found). Their first child, John, was born in about 1665. They had three more children: Henry, in about 1668 (probably named after his grandfather Henry), Alexander, born around 1670, and Rebecca, born around 1672.

They lived in a house on the grounds of a mill. The first mention of a

---

1   Miles, *Miles Files*. http://espl-genealogy.org/MilesFiles/site/index.htm. Descendants of Henry Bagwell 1.

mill on the Eastern Shore was in 1642. This mill was commissioned by Obedience Robins and Mr. Wilkins. A millwright, Anthony Lynney, set his hand and his seal to the agreement, "That the sayd Anthony Lynny should build sett upp and finish a Wyndemill within the county of Accomack for their use." The payment was "Two hundred and Twenty pounds sterling and Twenty Barrels of Indian Corne and to fynde all the iron worke of belonging and apperteyning unto the finishing of the said Mill."[2] Lynney also agreed to a date for completing the work and agreed not to take on any work until it was finished. Unfortunately for Robins and Wilkins, Anthony Lynney died before finishing the windmill. His inventory of goods and estate on April 28, 1642[3] has provided a list of his tools in the "working house":

> 3 whipp sawes, three tenant sawes and 3 handsawes, 10 agers, 1 gimblett, 4 paire of Chizell, more 2 gouges and 2 small Joyners Chizells, 13 Planes small and greate, 1 Froe piercers and one hammer, 1 pott and pott hookes, 2 broad Axes, 3 felling Axes and one Adds, 2 pestells made of old guns, one pick Axe, one paire of taylors shears, 2 small trays and one indian matt, fower trenchers and pewter porringer, 2 sifting trays, two old planeing iroms, a small prcell of old iron and sixe Sawwood Boards and old Grindlestone, 6 slabbs and a peece of a board.

Lynney had four servants and owned a house with a hall, a closet within the hall, and a "kitching." In the house were itemized two feather beds, a Bible, and three pictures in frames. He had a pistol, one looking glass, some small pewter pots, and Indian bowls and mats.

Mills at this time were for grinding grain into flour and cutting timber into planks. The miller was able to charge one sixth of the

---

2   Ames, *1640–1645 Acco-N II*, p. 155.

3   Ibid., p. 182.

weight of corn he ground.[4] Corn (maize) was the important staple for the families and, in 1647, the General Assembly made a law to protect the availability of corn. Every planter had to grow three acres of corn (land that was taxed) for each of his tithables. This was enforced by constables who visited the planters and checked that they kept to the law. The penalty was the loss of tobacco taken that year. This was good news for the owners of mills. Wind-powered mills have been found in Virginia from 1619 and have been described by Turman: "A small tower of bricks and wood held the wheels and belts which operated the grinding stones or saws while the large circular frame equipped with canvas strips harnessed the wind to turn the wheels."[5]

Unfortunately, the machinery of the mills sometimes exacted a toll on life or limb. It was an accident at the mill that brought a family tragedy to Henry and Alice and to their first grandson, John Bagwell, son of John and Ann. Records have stated that: "The death of John Bagwell, Junior was due to his being drawn between the cogwheel and trundle head of the mill belonging to his father."[6] He was about 16.

John Bagwell wrote his will on September 18, 1685 (see Appendix V). After his death, it was brought before the Open Court in Accomack County on November 30, 1686, and recorded and witnessed by John Washbourne, the clerk of the court, on December 8, 1686. It provides an interesting picture of the distribution of his land and property and the protection of the rights of his children, if his wife were to remarry. The will shows not only his ownership of his plantation, but part ownership of Cedar Island, of a mill and goods and chattels. His will also indicates that a "negro boy," whose name is not recorded, was to be passed on to his wife or to his daughter Rebecca.

4   Turman, *Eastern Shore*, p. 47.

5   Ibid., p. 47.

6   Ames, *Studies of the Eastern Shore*, p. 119.

The first Africans had arrived as captives in 1619 and many of them became workers on the plantations and in the homes of the early settlers, and were often identified in the wills of the settlers and in other records, censuses, and land patents.

Heywood and Thornton write: "Virginia's sparse African population is revealed as early as the census of 1620, taken after the first group of Africans arrived, which showed 32 of a population of 917 (3.5 per cent)."[7]

As has already been mentioned, the Eastern Shore has the oldest continuous records in the United States. The various census and court records have provided a source of information on white servants along with those of African descent who were living on the Eastern Shore at the same time that the Bagwell family were claiming their patent land on Old Plantation Creek. White indentured servants worked on the plantations. Ames says: "In the plantation system of Virginia such employment usually meant that the servant must till the soil, plant tobacco, and 'make corn' — labor absolutely essential to the livelihood and prosperity of the planter."[8]

Certainly John Clay, who was one of the named men, and whose transportation costs had been paid for by Henry Bagwell, must have stayed with Henry and would have gained his freedom after several years in that role.

John Bagwell's three remaining children are named in his will: Henry, Alexander, and Rebecca. Ann did marry again, to Edmund Allan, so she may have lost her rights to the profits of the water mill, which would have passed on to her children.

---

7   Heywood, Linda M., Thornton, John K., *Central Africans, Atlantic Creoles, and the Foundation of the Americas, 1585–1660* (New York, Cambridge University Press, 2007), p. 243.

8   Ames, *Studies of the Eastern Shore*, p. 76.

Rebecca Bagwell's story

As the daughter of Henry and Alice, Rebecca Bagwell mingled with the established families of the Eastern Shore; the church provided a place to meet and socialize with other young people and potential suitors. It was here that she probably met Robert Andrews, a son of Lt. Colonel William Andrews and his first wife Susannah. William was an Ancient Planter, had been a commissioner and vestryman, and represented Accomack at the House of Burgesses in 1641. He owned large tracts of land on Old Plantation Creek: 100 acres at Kings Creek, where Captain Epps' plantation was located, and 200 acres at Hungars Creek. He became a militia captain and later a major and was High Sheriff of Northampton in 1655.[9]

The marriage of Rebecca and Robert, which took place before 1656,[10] was important for the Bagwell family. Henry Bagwell and William Andrews were colleagues and had attended many court meetings together, as well as those at the vestry at Hungars Creek. It would have been a marriage attended by all the top families and a special day for Henry's young daughter. Robert Andrews died in 1657, and left his estate to his wife (with reversion to his nephews, William and Obedience Andrews), and 500 acres on Nandua Creek, which had been left to him by his father, William Andrews.[11]

Widows often sought a new spouse living in the immediate area.[12] The following year Rebecca Andrews married Stephen Fisher (born in 1636), who was the third son of John and Elizabeth Fisher, another established Eastern Shore family. Rebecca was expecting her first child in 1658, but feared that she would die in childbirth or that her child would die. She made a will as she needed to protect her property

9 McCartney, *Virginia*, p. 86.

10 Dorman, John Frederick, *Adventures of Purse and Person, Virginia, 1607–1624/5*, Vol. 1. Families A–F (Baltimore, Baltimore Genealogical Publishing Company Co, 4th edition, 2004), p. 92 (Bagwell Family).

11 Genealogy and History of the Eastern Shore. Snell. www.esva.net/ghotes.

12 Perry, *Formation of a Society*, p. 95.

and realized that her child would need the protection of guardians if she died.

The will also confirmed the members of her family and the importance of cattle for the planter family. Noted in an article under "A Window on Life and Death: Unborn Children" is the will of Rebecca Fisher, written on June 3, 1658:[13]

> To the childe now go with 10 cowes and 4 heifers. [The term "child now go with" refers to an unborn child and she is allocating the cattle to her child.]
>
> To my beloved sister Mary Hanby 2 cows and her daughters 2 heifers.
>
> To my well beloved brothers Thomas Stratton, John Bagwell and Thomas Bagwell. [She names her half- brother, Thomas Stratton and her two brothers but with no bequests.]
>
> To my brother Phillip Fisher one feather bed.
>
> To my brother Stratton's son Benjamin. [She also names Benjamin, the son of Thomas but again with no bequest.]
>
> To Rebecca, daughter of Tobias Selve my god-daughter one cow calf.
>
> To Hannah Wheeler a cow calf.
>
> If child I go with should die then the estate to be eq. divided by my own three brothers, sister Hanby and my brother Phillip Fisher.
>
> Brothers Thomas Stratton and Phillip Fisher overseers.
>
> Wit: *Elizabeth Selve, Agnes Stratton*

Family relationships are confirmed in her will: "Sister Mary Hanby" was her half-sister Mary, daughter of Alice (Chilcott) Bagwell. Phillip

---

13 Hickory House, *Oldest Continuous Records*, p. 17.

Fisher was the brother of Rebecca's second husband. She named in her will Rebecca Selve, the first child of Elizabeth (Chilcott) and Tobias Selve. Elizabeth Selve and Agnes Stratton, wife of Thomas Stratton, were the witnesses.

Rebecca gave birth to a girl, also named Rebecca, on 3 June 1658. A few weeks after giving birth, on 28 June, she died, as she had feared, and her daughter was placed under the care of Phillip Fisher, Stephen's brother. Stephen Fisher had also died in 1658 in Northampton County as on July 28, 1658 Rebecca was named as an orphan of Stephen Fisher deceased.[14] He was just 22 years of age, and his untimely death would account for Rebecca's need to secure the future of her unborn child.

Thomas Bagwell's story

Thomas was born in 1642, and was the youngest of Henry and Alice's children. He married Ann Stockley, daughter of Francis and Joan (Hall) Stockley. They went on to have a large family with eight children: Thomas, John, Comfort, Elizabeth, Francis, William, Ann, and Vallance.

In April 1663, Thomas received 200 acres of land from the 400 acres previously patented by his father Henry in 1639, on Old Plantation Creek, which his brother John had deeded to him as his share of the land inherited from their father. In 1669 Thomas took out another deed in which an additional 50 acres on Old Plantation Creek was given to his brother John. In 1682 he applied for a warrant for a survey of 1,000 acres in Sussex County, Delaware, which was successful as this land was mentioned in his will.

Thomas died in 1690, and his will of April 15 was confirmed at the Accomack County Court on September 16 of that year, witnessed by Lt. Colonel John West, Major Edmond Bowman, Captain William

---

14 Dorman, *Adventures of Purse and Person*, p. 955 (Fisher Family).

Curtis, and Captain Geoffrey Nicholas Hacks. The County Court Clerk was again John Washbourne.

He nominated his wife, Ann, as his sole executrix. His six surviving children received allocations of land including some outside Virginia in the territory of Pennsylvania at a place called Horekill, Sussex County. The will is of interest in that it details how land could be described by the details and markers, such as the oak tree to an undefined place across a pasture. It also identifies an area for an orchard and further land on Cedar Island

Thomas leaves land to his son John: "... from the white oak tree p[er] the creek Side which I marked myself: and soe run through the great pasture with a strait Line to the head line." To his son Thomas: "... the rest of the Dividend of my land here to be equally devided and the Sd Tho to have Shaire in the orchard & likewise my part in Seder Island." Thomas also inherits 200 acres of land next to William Burton.

Thomas Bagwell's two daughters, Ann and Vallance Bagwell, are given an equal share of the island as long as they stay unmarried. They both inherit a featherbed and furniture and 225 acres. John inherits a negro woman called Sarah when he reaches eighteen. Two more daughters, Elizabeth (wife of William Tilney) and Comfort (wife of Perry Leatherbury) are named, along with his grandchildren: "Item I give to everyone of my grandchildren namely Comfort Tilney & Ann Tilney one Cow this Spring to them and their heirs for ever with their increase."

Each son, Thomas, William, Francis, and John, received a gun, with Thomas receiving his pistols and holster, and Francis a horse, with its colt designated to Vallance. As long as his wife did not remarry she was allowed to keep cattle on the land at Horekill and a horse called Old Crippen and any increase.

The land in Sussex County in Pennsylvania was later included in the state of Delaware. Thomas and Ann's children married into many of the established families of the Eastern Shore, some of whom remained in Accomack while others, such as William and Thomas, moved to their land in Sussex County.

This next generation and the children of his brother John Bagwell, all Henry Bagwell's grandchildren, are traced and their marriages and children are found in the next chapter.

Chapter 11
The Third Generation: Henry's Grandchildren

Henry and Alice Bagwell's two sons, John and Thomas, and their daughter Rebecca had many children between them. There were also several grandchildren from Alice's children from previous marriages: her son Thomas Stratton, and daughters Mary and Elizabeth Chilcott, were Henry's stepchildren. This chapter relates what is known about Henry and Alice's grandchildren.

Sons and daughters of John and Ann Bagwell

John and Ann Bagwell had four children: John, Henry, Alexander, and Rebecca. Young John was born in about 1665, and died before May 19, 1681 in the accident in the mill at his father's plantation.

Henry Bagwell (1668–1734)

John and Ann's oldest surviving son Henry was first married to a Miss Crippen (her first name has not been found), and secondly to Margaret Drummond. Henry and Margaret had three sons, John, Henry, and Thomas, and three daughters, Elizabeth, Tabitha, and Ann. When Henry wrote his will, in August 1734, he was in his early sixties, owned a plantation, water mill, and land on Metomkin Creek, which was in Accomack County, and 300 acres of the land called "Marsh and Hammocks."[1] The will confirmed the names of his children and a grandson, as well as the identification of his land with interesting detail of the water mills and his possessions, and once again has provided unique information about one man's assets in 1734.

Henry's eldest son, John, had died before January 1729 and left a widow, Keziah (Smith) and one son, Charles. The administration of his estate was granted to Keziah by the Accomack Court.[2] An inventory of John's estate indicates that he was a shoemaker with tools, joiner's tools, sole leather, and a hide named in the list. He had a small number of cattle and pigs and one horse. He had a writing desk and an oval table, knives and forks, and some old chairs. One set of clothing is noted: a satin vest and breeches and one set of black stockings.

Henry itemizes in his will of 1734 what he is leaving to his eldest remaining son, the third Henry Bagwell. This included the 50 acres of land which was designated to his wife during her lifetime, and at the time was being used by another settler, Joseph Wimbrough. The land was described as:

> ... beginning at a pine on the North side of the Mill pond and thence running Northerly by a Line marked Trees to a little Branch and thence all the land on the north side of the said Branch up to the main road together with plantation whereon I now live

This was estimated to be about 150 acres. Henry also inherited part of a "Marsh and Hammocks lying on the South side of a Gut running out of the Bay into France Creek adjoining to the Marsh lately held by Thomas Simpson Senior deceased — containing — One hundred acres." Other items noted were a feather bed, furniture, and an old iron kettle.

---

1   Dorman, *Adventurers of Purse and Person*, p. 93 (Bagwell Family); Miles, *Miles Files*.
2   Nottingham, Stratton (ed.), *Wills and Administrations of Accomack County, Virginia 1663–1800* (Genealogical Co., Baltimore, 1999 [1931]), p. 104; Miles, *Miles Files*.

Thomas, the youngest son, inherited the plantation in Northampton County on Old Plantation Neck, which was 160 acres. He also received: "part of the Marsh and Hammock on the South side of Gut," estimated to be 150 acres. Thomas also inherited a feather bed and furniture. In addition he was to receive two cows, two year-old heifers, a black horse, and four sheep. Also noted were "Smith's tools."

In his will, Henry also mentioned Charles, the son of his deceased son John: "I Give to my said grandson Charles Bagwell his Heirs and Assigns for ever all the residue of my land lying on the Head of Matompkin Creek not already devised the same containing by Estimation One Hundred acres." This land at Metomkin in Accomack (see also Figure 8.1) and the creek with its inlet to the Atlantic coast is close to Cedar Island, which was also mentioned in the will of his father, John Bagwell, in 1685.

Items were left to his daughters, with Ann named as the main beneficiary. Ann inherited a feather bed and furniture and a cow calf but also a chest which had belonged to her grandmother (perhaps Alice Bagwell). In addition, she inherited a spinning wheel, slays and gears, and an interest in her father's horse, jointly with a man named Bowman Cropper. Her brother Thomas was instructed to give her and Tabitha £6 of Virginian money. Tabitha also inherited a spinning wheel. Elizabeth was already married to Isaac Rodgers and received a bed and bolster which had belonged to her mother.

Finally, Henry provided for his wife Margaret, but left clear expectations of her care of the property:

> I give and bequeath my loving Wife Margaret all the plantation whereupon I now live as it stands at present inclosed and also my Water Mill during her natural life and likewise full and free priviledge on any of my land thereto adjoining to get what timber She shall have occasion of for the repair of the said plantation and mill Except that part of my land whereupon my son Henry

now lives provided my said wife shall keep my said Mill in repair and when She shall fail to do so the same then my will is that the person to whom I shall hereafter devise the residuary Interest therein may enter and repair the said Mill and after such reparation made that my said wife shall only enjoy one third part of the profits therof as long as she live.

She also inherited a horse, plough, cart, and wheels.

The details of the will include many items of interest, showing the life of a third generation of a planter's family. His house on his plantation must have had many bedrooms as there were nine types of beds recorded. Some were old but two were "good beds" with bolsters weighing 37lbs, and estimated to be worth between £2 and £2.50 each. There was plenty of sheet linen, check linen, blankets, and pillows.

In the main living area there was an old desk, four chests, two square tables and one oval table, and four New England chairs, valued at 6s. 8d. He owned a lot of pewter, including one tankard and two dozen spoons. He had drinking glasses and a case of knives and forks. There were three spinning wheels for linen, one for wool, and a loom.

Many animals are named in the inventory, where horses appear to have the highest value. There was one young horse, and a breeding horse valued at £3 7s. 6d. This horse was probably the one identified in his will, and was a shared investment with another man called Bowman Cropper. He also owned six more horses with a total value of £5 5s. There were 18 sheep, plus cattle, pigs, and an old horse. There was a plough and grinding stones. He owned bellows for an anvil and this, with his smith's tools, was valued at £6. Shoemaker's tools were valued at 8s. 4d., and "upper leather" was valued at 8s. He may have been a shoemaker or employed a person as a blacksmith for the plantation.

Among his personal items were two pairs of spectacles, an old Bible, two razors, and a case. Clothes included a coat, jacket, and breeches at £1 10s. and several other coats and a beaver hat at 8s. He had 23 gallons of molasses and a barrel, and 10 barrels of Indian corn, valued at £2 10s.

A very interesting item described an investment of a "sixteenth part of sea sloop." His contribution was assessed as £5. There was also a sum of £6 1s. 3d. in the house. Ames' book on the Eastern Shore gives many interesting descriptions of the types of ships and small boats, the early industries, the shoemakers, and cattle industry present on the Eastern Shore during these years, as well as how the planters were self-sufficient on their plantations.[3]

This will of 1734 also mentions a "negro" called Jack, who would have helped with general duties on the plantation and in the home. Many of the first planters on the Eastern Shore had needed a considerable number of men to work in the plantation's tobacco fields. The first Africans who had been transported to Virginia in 1619 worked in the tobacco fields. Some of the planters on the Eastern Shore with many acres of land were owners of slaves; these planters included Charles Harmar, the Reverend William Cotton, and Colonel Edmund Scarburgh.[4] Ames notes that the local Native Americans also worked for the planters:

> In some instances the Indian was an indentured servant and, in others, a slave. During many years of the seventeenth century, there did not seem in practice a clear line of cleavage, the word *slave* occasionally being used when actually the status was that of an indentured servant.[5]

English indentured servants and others, who worked for three to

3   Ames, *Studies of the Eastern Shore*, pp. 111–146 passim.
4   Ibid., pp. 72–110 passim.
5   Ibid., p. 72

seven years for the man who had paid the costs of their passage under the "headright" system, could gain their own freedom to claim land.

Henry's second son, Henry, sadly died the year after his father, and his will was written on June 3, 1735, with his inventory confirmed by Accomack County on November 4, 1735.[6] He was married to Sabra who was the executor of the will. He named two sons, Heli and Spencer, and passed on the land left by his father Henry. Heli inherited the land and plantation and 50 acres; Spencer inherited the water mill and the "Marsh and Hammocks" and 150 acres. This mill and one miller had been mentioned in the will of John Bagwell, in 1685.

Henry's will of 1735 has some interesting items: a small flute, grains of silver, 7 pounds of nails at 6d. per pound, valued at 4s. 6d. There is a mention of 9 feet of window glass at 9s. 6d., wooden platters, and one spinning wheel. Once again his horse has the highest value at £4 10s., and he owned a small canoe valued at 4s.

Alexander Bagwell (1670–1722)

John and Ann's second son, Alexander, married firstly Elizabeth (no surname found) and secondly, Neomy Maddox. They had five daughters, Mary, Rebecca, Sarah, Anne, and Margaret. When Alexander died in 1722, in Northampton County, he left his wife a plantation in Metomkin, in Accomack County, part ownership of the water mill, and half of a marsh at the mouth of Guilford Creek. To his brother Henry, he left silver shoe buckles. He left silver spoons to his daughters, Rebecca, Sarah, and Anne. Mary and Margaret with their mother inherited the remaining estate.

Alexander also owned a woman called Judy who had a child and

---

6   Nottingham, *Wills and Administrations of Accomack County, Virginia 1663–1800*, p. 104.

was itemized in the will: "To wife n. woman Judy, and her child to my daughter, but if my daughter Mary dies under 18 then the n. to be equally div by the rest of my children."[7]

Rebecca (1672–1719)

John and Ann's daughter, Rebecca, married Thomas Mills (who died in 1709). There were six children of this marriage: Edmond, Thomas, Alexander, Elizabeth, Ann, and William Mills. She married again to Charles Stockley (who died in 1718), the son of John and Ann Stockley.

Daughter of Rebecca Bagwell

Rebecca Bagwell had been married twice, firstly to Robert Andrews and secondly to Stephen Fisher, whose family had lived on the Eastern Shore for many years. Rebecca and Stephen had one daughter, also named Rebecca, born on June 2, 1658. Rebecca was orphaned with the early death of both parents and was taken into the care of Stephen's brother, Captain Phillip Fisher.

Rebecca married William Walton before 1679 and they had four sons, John, Fisher, William, and Stephen, and moved to Somerset County, Maryland. After her husband died in 1686, she married Roger Odene, who had one son, Thomas.

The children of Thomas and Ann Bagwell

Thomas and Ann Bagwell's eight children[8] grew up on the Eastern Shore and married into established families, many moving to Sussex County.

Comfort married Perry Leatherbury, son of Thomas and Eleanor.

---

7   Marshall, James Handley (ed.), *Abstracts of the Wills and Administrations of Northampton County, Virginia, 1632–1802* (New England History Press, 1994), p. 242.

8   Genealogy and History of the Eastern Shore. Sussex County Delaware Records. www.esva.net/ghotes.

Comfort and Perry had seven children between 1686 and 1709: Perry, Edmund, Charles, Thomas, Comfort, Patience, and Ann. Comfort married again to Robert (Spencer) Burton.

William married Elizabeth Powell of Sussex County and had three children: Agnes, William, and Ann.

Elizabeth first married William Tilney, son of Colonel John Tilney. They had three children: Comfort, Patience, and Elizabeth. Elizabeth's second marriage was to James Davis, who died before June 2, 1713.

Francis first married Catherine Burton, daughter of Robert Spencer Burton and Catherine Cotton, and then married Susannah.

Ann married Griffiths Savage, and they had one daughter, Bridget.

Vallance married Charles Leatherbury and had five children: Thomas, John, Perry, Ann, and Elizabeth.

John married Tabitha Scarburgh, daughter of Colonel Charles Scarburgh, and they had three children.

Thomas married Elizabeth Eyre, daughter of John and Elizabeth from Sussex County, Delaware, and they had six children: Thomas, John, Susannah, Ann, Comfort, and Sarah.

Thomas and Agnes Stratton's children and descendants

Henry's stepson Thomas Stratton had married Agnes Johnson (Barnes) and they had two children, Ann and Benjamin.

Ann Stratton's story

Ann married William Burton. They had a large family: one daughter, Agnes (who married Edward Revell), and nine sons, William, Thomas,

Stratton, John, Benjamin, Joseph, Woolsey, Jacob, and Samuel.

William Burton died in 1695, leaving Ann a widow with all her sons under 21. William had invested in land and when he died was living in a place known as Forked Neck.

The nine sons inherited large tracts of land from their father, three of them in Accomack County, Virginia, two in Somerset County, Maryland, and four in Sussex County, Delaware. These extracts are from the will of William Burton:

> William: land on the sea-board side of Forked Neck where I now live.
>
> John: 500 acres in Sussex County, Pennsylvania, granted to me by patent.
>
> Benjamin: 600 acres in Assateague, sea-side side; other half of (1,000 acres) conveyed to me by Thomas Bagwell of Accomac.
>
> Joseph: 387 acres on the north side of Indian River, Sussex County.
>
> Woolsey: 387 acres being half of the said tract.
>
> Jacob: 450 acres near Lewis Town in Pennsylvania and adjacent to land given to John.
>
> Samuel: 500 acres on the south side of Indian River.
>
> To William, Thomas and Stratton — my interest in Cedar Island, Accomac.[9]

Ann married again to James Alexander.

One of Ann's sons, Woolsey Burton, born on February 20, 1688, built a brick house in 1717, which is known as the White House Farm, and still stands today on the northern bank of Indian River,

---

9   Nottingham, Stratton, *Accomack County Court Orders and Administrations, 1663–1680* (Bowie, Maryland, Heritage Books, 1990), p. 25.

on Long Neck. This was on land granted to William Burton Senior in 1677, by Governor Edmund Andross, representing the Duke of York. It is known locally as the White House Farm.

Woolsey had moved north to Indian River Hundred, Sussex County, circa 1705 from Accomack County, Eastern Shore, Virginia, to live on 387 acres that had been purchased by his father, William Burton. By the time of his death in 1730 he had acquired more than 3,000 acres. Woolsey's wife Ann survived her husband and inherited his land, becoming one of the few women landowners with extensive acres in the region. She remarried John Plasket, but after her death was buried next to Woolsey at the White House Farm, which is still owned by a descendant.[10] Their headstones remain there.[11]

Benjamin Stratton's story

Thomas and Agnes' second child, Benjamin, was born on February 25, 1657. He married Ann Wilkins, daughter of Nathanial Wilkins and Frances Hunt. Benjamin and Ann had five children: Agnes, Ann, Benjamin Junior, Nathaniel, and John. When Benjamin died on October 22, 1717, only two of the children had survived: Benjamin and John. Their daughter Agnes had died but she left two children, Benjamin and Ann Johnson.

Benjamin Junior inherited Stratton Manor (see Figure 11.1), "erected perhaps in its first version as early as 1694 by his father, on the land patented by Thomas Stratton in 1654, for his and his mother's adventure to Virginia in 1628."[12] In 1784, Benjamin Junior left the property to his son William Stratton with 585 acres. The property included:

> …. the main house, outbuildings, and the old kitchen all situated

---

10 Henry Bagwell entry at Wikitree.com, managed by Chet Snow. www.wikitree.com/wiki/Bagwell-209.

11 Find a Grave, Memorial to Woolsey Burton. No 103193041. www.findagrave.com.

12 McCurdy, "The English Origins," p. 16.

on Old Plantation creek. The creek appears as a boundary in a description of the property in a Northampton County land patent as early as 1654 when Thomas Stratton acquired 257 acres on what was then "Old Plantation Creek." The nominated acreage parallels the creek on the north, south, and west and is partially bounded on the east by an open field that has provided a dramatic setting for the house since the 18th century.[13]

Figure 11.1 Stratton Manor Marker. Courtesy of Northampton Historic Preservation Society.

13 United States Department of Interior, Heritage and Conservation and Recreation Service, *National Register of Historic Places Inventory; Stratton Manor*. Original date registered, 1940; Inventory 1958 (11 Nov 1980).

The land has been continuously farmed since the seventeenth century.

The children of Mary (Chilcott) and Richard Hanby II

Alice Bagwell's elder daughter Mary from her second marriage had two daughters with her husband Richard.

Rebecca, born circa 1660 in Northampton County, married Simon Thomas, a carpenter. Her father left her one cow in his will.

Elizabeth was born circa 1662 in Northampton County. She married William Scott I, son of Thomas and Ann Scott, and also inherited a feather bed from her father.

The children of Elizabeth (Chilcott) and Tobias Selve (Selby)

Alice Bagwell's younger daughter, Elizabeth, from her second marriage had four daughters with her husband Tobias.

Clemency, born circa 1650, married John Smalley.

Elizabeth, born circa 1655, married William Fletcher.

Matilda, born circa 1658, married Arnold Harrison.

Rebecca, born circa 1655, remained unmarried.

Chapter 12

The Other Bagwell, Burgess for Pasbehay, 1625

There was another Bagwell in Virginia who was noted in the census of 1625 in the household of Henry Bagwell and in records of the courts. This was Thomas Bagwell of Pasbehay. Henry Bagwell had named his second son Thomas, and also a grandson had been named Thomas, but the records of Exeter have provided the detail of Henry's brothers and sisters and they did not include a Thomas.[1]

In Virginia, Thomas Bagwell was given the status of Ancient Planter, a person who arrived in Virginia before May 1616. His actual arrival and the name of his ship have not been recorded.

Thomas was certainly with Henry in 1624 and on February 16 was recorded as living at West and Shirley Hundred. "By February 4th, 1625, he had moved to the Neck of Land where he headed a household that had a modest supply of stored food and defensive weapons," says McCartney.[2] In 1624, there were twenty-five people living here with at least four households, but this had declined to seventeen by 1625. One of the people living here at this time was an African servant named Edward.[3]

Thomas married the widow of Thomas Allnutt, who had arrived on the *Gift*. Thomas Allnutt had lived on the mainland behind

---

1   St. Petrock's Parish Records.

2   McCartney, *Virginia*, p. 100.

3   Ibid., p. 38.

Jamestown, within the neck of land where he had a patent for some land. By 1625 he had a house and boat, but by August 21, 1626 he had died, leaving Ann a widow. She quickly remarried Thomas Bagwell in February 1627. McCartney reports that he became a burgess for Pasbehay, known as the Governor's Land:

> Throughout the colonial period, the 3,000 acre tract known as the Governor's Land was reserved for the use of the colony's highest official. Most governors leased portions of their office land to tenants but placed their own servants upon the property.[4]

In 1638, Thomas Bagwell had 450 acres of land in Charles City: "In Apamattuck Riv, S upon a Cr, N towards Conjurors field, E upon the river and W. into the maine woods. 100 acres due for his wife Joane and 300 acres for trans. of 6 persons."[5]

In 1645, at the court hearing of 4 July, Thomas Bagwell signed his mark, as a witness to Henry Bagwell's gift to Jane Williams:

> These present witnesset That I Henry Bagwell doe give unto Jane Williams the daughter of Henry Williams one Cowe Calfe Browne Colloured upper Bitten on the left eare and under bitten of the right eare with one heele[?] in on the Age of three Moneths at the date hereof which Cowe Calfe withy her increase to remayyne for the only use of th said Jane. To which present guift I the said Henry Bagwell have put to my hand the 25th May 1645.

> *Henry Bagwell*[6]
> In the presents of
> The marke of *Richard Smyth*
> *Thomas Bagwell* Recordatur 4th die mensis July 1645
> *Per Edwynn Conaway, Clericus Curiae*[7]

---

4   Ibid., p. 37.
5   Nugent, *Cavaliers and Pioneers*, Vol. 1, p. 87.
6   Ames, *1640–1645 Acco-N II*, p. 429.
7   Ibid., p. 249.

Both Henry and Thomas Bagwell made their mark on the settlement of Virginia. Both became burgesses and represented the other settlers at the meetings of the Assembly in Jamestown. They were both active in the affairs of Virginia at the same time, and both invested in land.

Chapter 13

Henry's Friends and Neighbors on the Eastern Shore

Henry was a prominent person on the Eastern Shore and many of the early settlers were his friends and colleagues: men like William Epps and Thomas Graves, as the first commanders for Accomack; the traders Henry Fleet, William Clayborne, and Charles Harmar; and those involved in the political world, such as Obedience Robins, John Wilcocks, and Edmund Scarburgh. Each of these men would leave their imprint and stories, and aspects of their lives can be traced through the records of the courts.

It was a very small community in 1625. These men met at the various gatherings of the General Assembly in Jamestown, the monthly meetings of the court at Accomack, and the vestry. They all lived along the creeks of the Eastern Shore.

Each had a different role in the early days of the colony and most of them stayed in Virginia, accessed land by patent, and brought up their families. They, like Henry Bagwell, were pioneers and adventurers. They left their mark on the Eastern Shore of Virginia and England's first permanent colony in the New World.

William Epps (1595–1641)

William Epps came from Ashford in Kent to Virginia on the *William and Thomas* in 1618. His wife Margaret came on the *George* in 1621. He was an agent and took care of the settlers in Smyth's (Southampton) Hundred. In 1625 he was living on his plantation with Margaret and 13 servants. His plantation was next to Old Plantation Creek and had two dwellings, three storehouses, and a palisade. He was brought before the General Court for bad behavior: "an affront to public morality."[1] He left Virginia for the West Indies and was a member of the council for St. Christopher's, but returned to Ashford, Kent, in 1630.

Thomas Graves (c. 1580–1635)

Thomas was an Ancient Planter like Henry Bagwell. He was awarded 200 acres and £25 for his investment in the Virginia Company.[2] At the Assembly of 1629 he was named as a burgess. By 1632, as Captain Graves, he was one of the four named burgesses for Accomack with Captain Edmund Scarburgh, Obedience Robins, and Henry Bagwell. Graves became a commissioner and was a member of the vestry.

Obedience Robins (1601–1662)

In 1632, Obedience was the first commander of the monthly court with the first commissioners, who were Captain William Clayborne, Captain Thomas Graves, John Howe, Gentleman, Captain Edmund Scarburgh, Roger Saunders, Gentleman, and Charles Harmer, Gentleman.

Robins was a successful politician and businessman. He commissioned the first mill in 1641 with his partner, John Wilkins, and they paid a millwright, Anthony Lynney, £220 sterling and 20 barrels of corn.[3] This was probably the mill owned by John Bagwell. In 1634 he became the county's deputy-lieutenant.

---

1 McCartney, *Virginia*, p. 283.
2 Ibid., p. 337.
3 Wise, *Ye Kingdome*, p. 293.

The signatures of Obedience Robins and Henry Bagwell can be found on the minutes of the meeting of the Accomack court on September 17, 1633.

Robins combined public office with private enterprise, and agriculture with trade for social and economic security.[4] Henry and Obedience would have met many times during their attendance at the court during the years 1632 to 1640 where Henry, as clerk, recorded the decisions made by Obedience and the other commissioners. As Mary Catherine Wilheit observes:

> Court meetings and attendant duties demanded sacrifice and dedication from commissioners who concomitantly promoted their own interests, furthered by their familiarity with the parameters of colonial regulation. Local courts became effective instruments of government and self-interest.[5]

Obedience had a 35-year career and involvement with the administrative system and became an influential member of the Eastern Shore gentry.

Ensign Thomas Savage (1594–1631)

Thomas was in the First or Second Supply convoy of ships which arrived in Virginia in 1608. He went to live with the Native American tribe of Powhatan. Thomas stayed with them for three years, became fluent in their language, and gained a knowledge of their customs. He traded actively with the Indians, who gave Savage some land on the Eastern Shore. In 1632 he obtained a 21-year lease for 100 acres on Old Plantation Creek. He had died by 1633 as his wife Hannah was named as a widow at this time and their son John inherited the land.[6]

---

4   Wilheit, M.C., "Obedience Robins of Accomack: 17th Century Strategies for Success," MA Thesis, Texas A&M University, submitted December 1997. Abstract, iii.

5   Ibid., p. 75.

6   McCartney, *Virginia*, p. 624.

John later married Mary, daughter of Obedience Robins. Hannah Savage later married Daniel Cugley, whose inventory was examined in 1641 and from whom Henry Bagwell bought some items.

Captain Henry Fleet (1602–1661)

Henry was a neighbor of John Blower and Thomas Savage who, in 1626, along with Sir George Yeardley, were the only three people who held patents on the Eastern Shore. Savage's tracts, according to Ames, "abutted on the land of Captain Fleete and that in turn was adjacent to the land patented by Henry Bagwell."[7]

In March 1628 Captain Fleet was granted 100 acres of land "under the yearly rent of one shillings for every Fifty acres."[8] He was captured by the Native Americans while trading on the Potomac River and lived with them for five years but, after a ransom was paid, returned and patented land on the Eastern Shore. He created a trading partnership with the Indian villages and, in 1646, he negotiated a peace treaty with the Indians.[9]

He returned to England and became involved with Cecil Calvert, Lord Baltimore, and helped him with land deals, which led to the building of St. Mary's City, the first capitol of Maryland. He was an important trader. He became a burgess and a lieutenant colonel in the militia and died around 1661.

Charles Harmar (1600–1640)

Charles was named as the overseer for Lady Dale's land and, by 1626, had gained a patent of 100 acres in his own right and a further 1,000 acres in the 1630s. He was accorded the title "Gentleman" and was one of the first commissioners for Accomac. He also was an early

---

7   Ames, *1640–1645 Acco-N II*, p. 22.
8   Ibid., p. 15.
9   McCartney, *Virginia*, p. 303.

owner of African slaves:

> In 1635 among the eight negro headrights of Charles Harmar was one of the name of John, and in 1640 Nathaniel Littleton, who had married Ann, the widow of Charles Harmar, acknowledged for himself, his heirs and assigns, that Garret Andrews had previously bought the negro John from Ann for 1,200 pounds of Tobacco.[10]

There is an additional statement that provides another interesting detail of this aspect of life in the colony and the life and ownership of the black slaves. Harmar had two slaves imported in 1635, Ames writes: "namely Anthony and Cassango. Among the twenty-three negroes bequeathed in 1636 by Harmar's widow, Ann Littleton, were the son of old Anthony and Cassango and her two children."[11] The passing on of slaves to family members was noted in the Records of Accomack-Northampton and in many wills. Says Ames:

> The fact that some of those negroes and their children were still in the possession of the family of the man who brought them to Virginia more than two decades earlier would seem to strengthen the theory of slavery rather than servitude.[12]

William Clayborne (1600–1666)

William came to Virginia in 1621 and became the first surveyor of Virginia. His first assignment was to lay out public lands for private individuals who would pay him in tobacco for his services.[13]

In 1627 he surveyed and recorded the first lands on the Shore, when he came to look after the secretary's land. In 1629 he was sent to England by the Jamestown government to report to investors and

10 Ames, *1640–1645 Acco-N II*, p. 105.
11 Ibid., p. 105.
12 Ibid., p. 105.
13 Turman, *Eastern Shore*, p. 10.

other people with an interest in Virginia, about a visit to Virginia from Lord Baltimore. There was a suspicion that Lord Baltimore was attempting to acquire land in Virginia. This turned out to be true and King Charles I finally signed a charter for this land, which became Maryland. In 1632, the patent was passed on to Cecil Calvert, Lord Baltimore's son and heir, but Virginia had maintained control of the entrance to Chesapeake Bay.

The General Assembly had met on July 5 and in September 1632. Henry Bagwell attended both of these meetings, and at the September meeting, Captain William Clayborne was appointed commander. By 1634, Clayborne had been appointed lieutenant for Accomack and secretary. He was forced out of this latter role by Governor Harvey, who was himself displaced in the following year. However, Harvey returned in 1636 but was still opposed by members of the Council of State. They disliked his authoritarian way of governing the colony. It was a time of turmoil.

William went on to be a leading merchant and formed key partnerships with London merchants William Cloberry, Maurice Thompson, and William Tucker, who would all be involved in developing trading opportunities in Maryland, based on Kent Island. These men would develop many syndicates over the next 20 years and gain a monopoly on trade in the colonies.

Edmund Scarburgh (1584–1635)

He came to Virginia prior to March 1630, from Norfolk. He held office as a burgess to 1633 and served as a commissioner at the local court. He was named as a burgess with Henry at the first meeting of the General Assembly called by Governor Harvey at the February meeting of 1630. He lived at Magothy Bay and had a large number of cattle.

His son Edmund (1617–1671) succeeded him. He used his parents as his headrights to gain land and would become a leading personality over the next few years. He was in charge of the Magothy Bay area when Accomack (now named Northampton) was divided into military districts as directed by Sir William Berkeley, governor and captain general of Virginia. He rose through the ranks, from burgess to Speaker of the House in 1645, justice for Northampton, and surveyor-general of Virginia in 1655. His sons followed the same pathway. His daughter Hannah married John Wise of Devonshire and founded the Wise family of the Eastern Shore.

Jennings Cropper Wise, historian of the Eastern Shore, described him as a "warm hearted, fearless, pugnacious, enterprising man, highly educated, and equal of any Virginian of his day as a soldier, scholar, or useful citizen."[14]

John Wilcocks

John was from Exeter, Devon, and came to Virginia on the *Bona Nova* in 1620. In the 1625 census he was living on the Eastern Shore as a free man.

John applied for 500 acres at Old Plantation Creek but, by January 1621, had drowned while crossing the Chesapeake Bay. It was noted that he had property in Plymouth and New England when his will was presented for probate.[15]

---

14 Wise, *Ye Kingdome*, p. 86.
15 McCartney, *Virginia*, p. 746.

From the Old World to the New

The founder of this family in America was Henry Bagwell, believed to have been a native of Devonshire, who, as a member of Admiral Summers' Expedition went to America from Bermuda in the Deliverance in 1608 and settled in Accomack County, Virginia.

—*Burke's American Families with British Ancestry*[1]

Henry's early years were spent in Exeter, a city where successful merchants could live with their families in fine houses in the High Street, with many rooms, rich furniture and fittings, glass in their windows, large kitchens and storehouses for food, and small gardens. They could afford the best silver, have books and Bibles and expensive clothes. They had shops and warehouses and "bartons," houses in the country where they kept chickens, pigs, and horses. They could buy land and invest in houses; they could support some of the early explorations with donations of money, and invest in shipping.

The Chappell family was one such family. The men rose to prominence during the Tudor period and became important civic figures, successful merchants, and family men with large households. Details of their lives have been documented in the ancient records of the city, in wills and inventories and written evidence of the early historians of Exeter. Their deaths at a time when their children were very young, and the need for their assets to be detailed by the

---

1 *Burke's Genealogical and Heraldic History of the Landed Gentry, including American Families with British Ancestry* (London, Burke's Peerage, 1939 [1826]), p. 2544.

Exeter Orphans' Court, have left unique records. This was true for William Chappell, Thomas Chappell, and sadly for David Bagwell, the father of Henry Bagwell.

Henry was 14 when his father died in an accident at sea, near the port of St. Malo on the French coast. His mother married again, to John Parr, and Henry would have been under his care until he was 21. However, in 1609, at the age of 20, Henry was ready for adventure and free to seek the opportunities offered in the New World.

This story has followed his footsteps from England to Virginia, an epic voyage with a storm, shipwreck, survival on an island, and subsequent arrival in Jamestown to his first home on the West and Shirley Plantation. From here he voyaged down the James River and across Chesapeake Bay to his permanent residence in Accomack, on Old Plantation Creek, on Virginia's Eastern Shore.

Traces

Exeter

St. Petrock's Church, where Henry was christened, still stands at the bottom of Exeter High Street. The fourteenth-century church of St. Olave, where Henry's father David was buried, and where French Protestants could worship between 1635 and 1758, is still tucked in between the buildings in Fore Street. The Chappell houses of 41 and 42 High Street are hidden behind the fascia of a modern shop but still contain the remains of Tudor fireplaces, and a side oven from the sixteenth century, with painted decorations and a partial image of a young man with a hawk on his left hand.[2]

---

2   Thorpe, J.R.L., recordings by Exeter Archaeology (1976), later published in Allan, John, Alcock, Nat, and Dawson, David, *West Country Households 1500–1700*, Monograph 9 (Woodbridge and New York, Society for Post-Medieval Archaeology, Boydell Press, 2015), Chapter 6.

Further down Fore Street stands Tuckers Hall, built and owned by the Guild of Weavers, Tuckers and Shearmen since 1471. Here the merchants met and regulated the woollen cloth trade, an industry that brought great wealth to Exeter. The guild was incorporated in 1620 with a royal charter and became the Incorporation of Weavers, Fullers and Shearmen. Members of the Chappell and Bagwell families would have spent many hours in this building; the 800-year-old Guildhall, the center for all civic activities, is still standing, as well as the remains of a castle, Rougemont, St. Nicholas Priory, and many Tudor buildings and ancient churches.

This is the city where Henry's parents, David Bagwell and Johane Chappell, were married, had their first home, and raised their family. Henry grew up here, in a city wealthy with the profits of the wool trade, with a canal built in 1566 to provide access for ships on the river Exe and links to the town of Topsham at the mouth of the river.

The Sea Venture

Wrecked on the reefs of Bermuda in 1609, the *Sea Venture* has survived in the form of some of its timbers. In 1958, Edmund Downing, an amateur diver, was the first to discover ballast stones and timbers of an old wreck. He was joined by Bob and Donald Canton and Teddy Tucker, and more investigations took place. Due to a wrong diagnosis about the date of a cannon, however, the ship was thought not to be the *Sea Venture*. It would take another 20 years before the next search took place. Allan J. Wingood, a retired professional diver and member of the newly formed Bermuda Maritime Museum Association, took over the responsibility for the next excavation. Artifacts were recorded, photographed, and researched. His report indicated that there were many exciting finds including weapons, household items, a pewter candlestick, and fragments of pottery from Bideford and Barnstaple.[3] Wingood noted that such pottery was also found at Martin's Hundred in Virginia and at Jamestown.

Exploration has continued with Dr. Philippe Rouja, Bermuda's Custodian of Historic Wrecks, who has not only led many dives but also a project with the University of California, San Diego, in which 3D images from the dives were made. In 2014, a 50-minute film was made, *Downing's Wreck—The Story of the Sea Venture.*[4]

Other traces of Henry's journey can be found in the historic St. George's Parish, a UNESCO World Heritage Site. In 2011, a memorial was built overlooking the area where the *Sea Venture* ran aground, to celebrate the survivors of the 1609 shipwreck. On one plaque can be found the name of Henry Bagwell and once a year there is a celebration organized by the St. George's Foundation when the names of those survivors are read out.[5]

A replica of the *Deliverance,* the ship which was built by Sir Thomas Gates to take the survivors on to their destination at Jamestown, stands on Ordnance Island, located in St. George's. In the memorable words of author Avery Kolb:

E1 The Memorial Cross in Bermuda to celebrate the survivors of the *Sea Venture.*

3   Wingood, A.J., "*Sea Venture*: An interim report on an early 17th century shipwreck lost in 1609," *International Journal of Nautical Archaeology and Underwater Exploration*, 1982, 11(4), 333–347.

4   Look Bermuda/Look Films, *Downing's Wreck—The Story of the Sea Venture.* www.lookbermuda.com/seaventure.

5   www.stgeorgesfoundation.org.

The story of the British ship *Sea Venture* is one of history's most remarkable sagas, an almost unbelievable tale of shipwreck, endurance, and human resourcefulness. But it is more than that. The fate of the survivors of the *Sea Venture* reverberates in literature, in political theory — in the very founding of America.[6]

In a recent book, *Marooned*, historian Joseph Kelly offers a fresh interpretation of the Virginia colony, opining that the founding of America should be celebrated with the survival of those men and women on the *Sea Venture*, shipwrecked in 1609 on Bermuda:

> Our true birth was a plunge and a forgetting: wrecking on the rocks, sinking in the brine, floating away from solid decks, loosed from the timbers of the Old World, set loose from old bindings, stumbling ashore drenched and dripping. The salvage begins, Americans are castaways, and we began on a reef in the mid-Atlantic.[7]

Those men on the *Sea Venture*, Sir Thomas Gates, Sir George Somers, Captain Christopher Newport, Sir George Yeardley, John Rolfe, and Reverend Richard Bucke, were the nucleus of officials who would all play important roles in the securing a future for Jamestown and thus England's first permanent colony in the New World.

Other influential men were William Strachey, the first Secretary for the Virginia Council, whose eyewitness account of the shipwreck and early days of the colony may have inspired the opening scenes of Shakespeare's play *The Tempest*. Strachey's chronicle was not officially published until 1625, however, as the Virginia Company of London feared his descriptions would deter future investors. Sylvester Jourdaine's account, printed in 1610, was seen to be more favorable.

6 Kolb, Avery, "The Tempest."
7 Kelly, *Marooned*, p. 22.

Jamestown

When Henry first arrived at Jamestown in 1610, he was one of the survivors of the *Sea Venture* shipwreck, and, with the other colonists, worked under Sir Thomas Gates and Sir Thomas Dale to restore the buildings in Jamestown and bring some order to the struggling colony.

Since 1994, the Jamestown Rediscovery Project with Preservation Virginia, under the leadership of William M. Kelso and James Horn, has systematically uncovered and revealed what remains of the first settlement.

E2 The Jamestowne Society's Registered Mark. The author wishes to express her appreciation to the Jamestowne Society for granting her written permission to use the Jamestowne Society's registered mark (P.O. Box 6845, Richmond, Virginia, 23230).

They have unearthed cobblestones, the outlines of houses, postholes 12 feet apart that match the historical records of a wooden church, and hundreds of other items. In 2014, they found buried in a cellar a partial skeleton of a young girl. Her bones were examined and traces of cannibalism were found, linking this find to the reported "starving time" of 1610–1611. Gravestones of the early colonists have been located, as well as a ring with the crest of William Strachey, and, in 2018, ten teeth, which helped researchers to understand the diet of those early settlers.

Kelso's *Jamestown: The Buried Truth* and *Jamestown, The Truth Revealed*[8] and the information produced in updates by the Jamestown Rediscovery Project[9] have documented the findings over the years, providing information on buildings and artifacts, and identifying some skeletons of the original inhabitants of James Fort.

---

8 Kelso, William M., *Jamestown, The Buried Truth* (Charlottesville, VA, University of Virginia Press, 2006); Kelso, William M., *Jamestown, The Truth Revealed* (Charlottesville, VA, University of Virginia Press, 2017).

9 Jamestown Rediscovery. https://historicjamestowne.org.

Henry was there and survived to help settle the New World. He is celebrated as a Jamestowne Qualifying Ancestor by the Jamestowne Society of Richmond.[10]

> Virginia was the first of England's settlements in America to persist and ultimately flourish. The great reforms of 1619 that took place at Jamestown had an enduring influence on the development of Virginia and British America and heralded the opening of an extended Anglo-American examination of sovereignty, individual rights, liberty, and constitutionalism that would influence all Britain's colonies.[11]

West and Shirley Hundred

As we have seen, Henry's first ownership of land in 1625 was 50 acres at a plantation at West and Shirley Hundred with his partner, Simon Sturgis. The plantation was named after two investors involved with the Virginia Company of London, Sir Thomas West, Lord de la Warr, and Sir Thomas Shirley, the father of Thomas West's wife. Situated on the north bank of the James River, this plantation is credited as the oldest in Virginia, established in 1614. It was where tobacco was grown and shipped to England and other colonies. McCartney comments that "collectively, the early records associated with West and Shirley Hundred reveal that life on the Virginia frontier was stressful and turbulent. The Indians harassed West and Shirley Hundred's inhabitants almost continuously until at least 1627."[12]

This may have caused Henry's move to the Eastern Shore.

---

10 www.jamestowne.org.
11 Horn, *1619 Jamestown and the Forging of American Democracy*, p. 10.
12 McCartney, *Virginia*, p. 57.

The Eastern Shore of Virginia

Henry became an important man in the emerging society of the Eastern Shore from the 1630s, and incidents in his life have been traced through the records, land patents, and evidence of the early historians of the Eastern Shore. His role as the first clerk of the County Court of Accomack-Northampton and his signature on the very first pages of the first continuous records of America can be celebrated and finally acknowledged.

E3 The Northampton County Court House, built in 1731. Northampton Historic Preservation Society.

Henry Bagwell's inheritance

Henry's inheritance can be measured in the survival of his children and grandchildren, who married into many of the other colonial families and whose descendants are many and spread out in numerous other areas of the United States. He and Alice also left a sizable inheritance in terms of land which they passed on to their children.

The Stratton inheritance

Alice (Stratton, Chilcott) Bagwell had been granted 200 acres for transporting herself and a son, Thomas, and two servants. She passed 100 acres to her son and to her daughter Mary Chilcott.

In 1654, Thomas patented a neck of land called Aqusca (later known as Joyner's Neck), which was 257 acres. The Stratton family continued to buy land and "possessed acreage extending entirely across the Shore, as well as acreage elsewhere."[13] This is the Thomas Stratton who married the widow, Agnes Barnes, previously named Johnson.

This is the land where Stratton Manor can be found, where a brick chimney has an old date, marked 1694, and another, dated "Benjamin Stratton 1764."

E4 Stratton Manor. Northampton Historic Preservation Society, with permission of the owner, Karl Wagner

13 Whitelaw, Ralph Thomas, *Virginia's Eastern Shore*, vol. 1 (Virginia Historical Society, 1951), p. 127.

The Chilcott inheritance

Henry's two stepdaughters were Mary and Elizabeth Chilcott.

Mary divorced her first husband, Richard Buckland, and married Richard Hanby, who in 1658 owned land in Baltimore County, Maryland, but sold this and returned to Northampton. They had two daughters, Rebecca and Elizabeth. Mary died during 1663 and Richard remarried Susanna Daniel. Rebecca married Simon Thomas and Elizabeth married William Scott I.

Elizabeth Chilcott married Tobias Selve who, in 1666, patented 600 acres of land, named tract A24, which was south of the town of Pungoteague in Accomack County. He bequeathed his land to his daughters, Clemency, Rebecca, Elizabeth, and Matilda.

The Bagwell inheritance

Historian Ralph Whitelaw made a study of the early land patents, which formed the content of his book, *Virginia's Eastern Shore*, published in 1951. He noted that Henry "... left no will and the date of his death is uncertain, but the title passed to John, as eldest son."[14] He confirmed that in 1663, John Bagwell deeded the southern 200 acres to his brother Thomas, but six years later, Thomas and Ann Bagwell deeded 50 acres of it back. Whitelaw researched the ownership of land which had been Henry's original 400 acres. This land, which had been divided between Henry's two sons, was identified as the "Thomas Bagwell Part" and "John Bagwell Part."

Thomas Bagwell Part: In 1667, 150 acres were sold to a John Michael by Thomas and Ann Bagwell (A66) of Metomkin and John and Ann Bagwell.

---

14 Whitelaw, *Virginia's Eastern Shore*, Vol. 1, p. 117.

John Bagwell Part: In 1669, John sold 250 acres to a John Waterson and the family of John Wilkins, as well as some acres which he and John Wilkins had accumulated over the years.[15]

The last trace of Henry Bagwell

The last mention of Henry was in November 1659 in the Northampton County, Virginia Record Book, Court Cases:

> It is ordered that Mr. Henry Bagwell be paid out of the estate of Wm Johnson dec'd the sum of 167 pounds of tobacco.
>
> Also another 70 pounds forthwith and 500 sixpenny nails.[16]

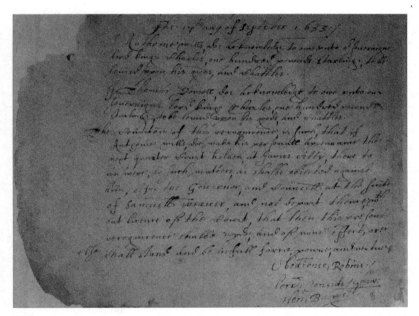

E5 Henry's signature. From the original held at Northampton County Court: Order Book No. 1, 1633. Bayside Transcriptions.

---

15 Ibid., p. 118
16 Mackay, Dr. Howard and Groves, Marlene A. (eds.), *Northampton County, Virginia Record Book, Court Cases, Vol. 8, 1657–1664*, 29 Jan 1658/59 Court (Maine, Picton Press, 2002), pp. 87 and 88. Courtesy of Miles Files.

Warren M. Billings, in his epilogue to *The Old Dominion in the Seventeenth Century*, states:

> Despite the high social costs inherent in the development of the Old Dominion, the seventeenth-century Virginians left succeeding generations of colonists an enduring patrimony. They passed on habits and experiences that their fellow countrymen would one day translate into fundamental rights upon which lay the foundation of a nation. And in the creation of that inheritance hangs the significance of Virginia's first century.[17]

Henry Bagwell was a castaway, survived a shipwreck, and was marooned on an island.

He was one of the first colonists on the mainland of Virginia.

He played important roles in the early years of the Eastern Shore of Virginia.

A family man.

An adventurer and planter.

A Virginian.

This is his story.

---

17 Billings, *The Old Dominion*, p. 324.

APPENDICES
Appendix I
Excester, the walled city

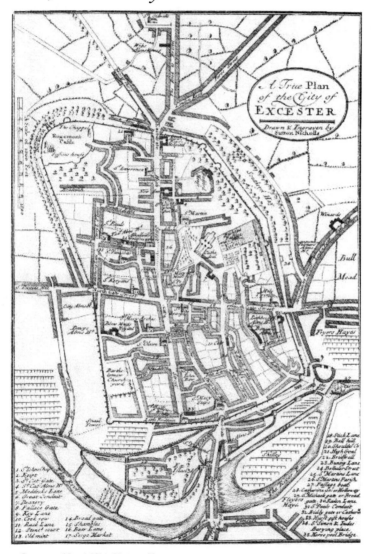

Courtesy of South West Heritage Trust.

Appendix II
Chappell and Bagwell Family Tree: Devon

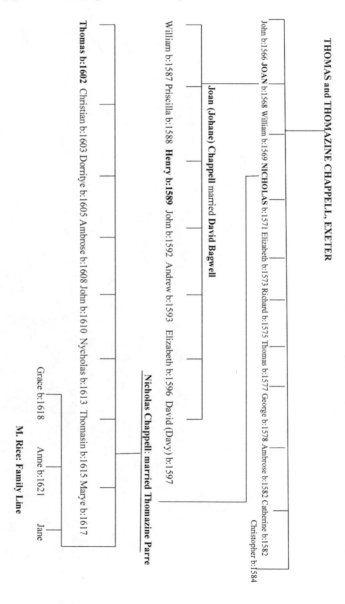

THOMAS and THOMAZINE CHAPPELL, EXETER

John b:1566 **JOAN** b:1568 William b:1569 **NICHOLAS** b:1571 Elizabeth b:1573 Richard b:1575 Thomas b:1577 George b:1578 Ambrose b:1582 Catherine b:1582

Christopher b:1584

Joan (Johane) Chappell married **David Bagwell**

William b:1587 Priscilla b:1588 **Henry b:1589** John b:1592 Andrew b:1593 Elizabeth b:1596 David (Davy) b:1597

Nicholas Chappell: married Thomazine Parre

Thomas b:1602 Christian b:1603 Dorritye b:1605 Ambrose b:1608 John b:1610 Nycholas b:1613 Thomasin b:1615 Marye b:1617

Grace b:1618   Anne b:1621   Jane

M. Rice: Family Line

Appendix III

Henry's Step-Family on Old Plantation Creek, Virginia

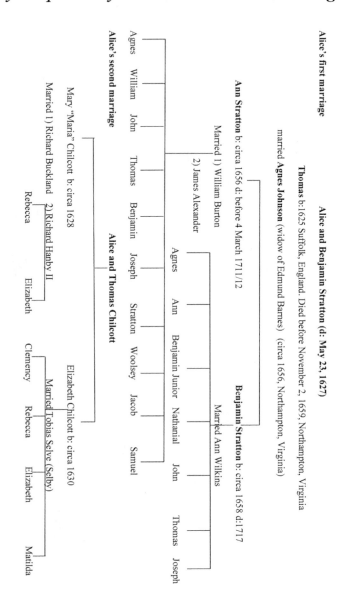

Appendix IV
Henry and Alice Bagwell's Family Tree

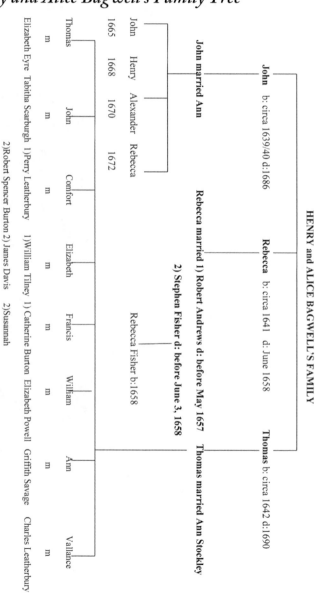

HENRY and ALICE BAGWELL'S FAMILY

John b: circa 1639/40 d:1686

John married Ann

John 1665
Henry 1668
Alexander 1670
Rebecca 1672

Thomas m Elizabeth Eyre
John m Tabitha Scarburgh
Comfort m 1)Perry Leatherbury
Elizabeth m 1)William Tilney 1) Catherine Burton
Francis m Elizabeth Powell
William m Griffith Savage
Ann m Charles Leatherbury
Vallance

2)Robert Spencer Burton 2) James Davis 2)Susannah

Rebecca b: circa 1641 d: June 1658

Rebecca married 1) Robert Andrews d: before May 1657

2) Stephen Fisher d: before June 3, 1658

Rebecca Fisher b:1658

Thomas b: circa 1642 d:1690

Thomas married Ann Stockley

Appendix V
John Bagwell's Will, September 18, 1685

At a Court held in Accomack County, Novem^ber ye 30th 1686

Lt. Coll Jn° West

Capt Wm Curtis Mr William Anderson

Lt Coll Danl Jenifer

In the name of God Amen the eighteenth day of September 1685 according to the computation of the Church of England I, John Bagwell of the County of Accomack in Virginia Cooper being of perfect memory and Remembrance Praised be God do make and ordaine this my last Will and Testam^t in manner & forme viz

First I bequeath my Soul into the hands of Almighty God my maker hoping that through the meritorious death and passion of Jesus Christ my onely Saviour and Redeemer to receive free pardon and forgiveness of all my sins and as for my body to be buried in Christian burial att ye discretion of my Executrx and Executrs hereafter nominated.

Item I give unto my Son Henery Bagwell ye one halfe of my planation I now live on with his equal share of my third part of an Island purchased with Thomas Bagwell and Isaac Medcalfe and myself also I give him one Featherbed with all furniture now belonging to it to be left in god condition as now it is: when my son shall attain eighteen years old & then he to be capable to enjoy his Estate Reall & personal also I give him one Gunn

Item I give unto my Son Alexander Bagwell ye other halfe of my Plantation I now live on w[i]^th his equal Share of my third part of an Island purchased by Thomas Bagwell and Isaac Medcalfe and myself also I give him one feathered bed with all furniture now belonging to

be left in good condition as now it is when my said son shall attain eighteen years old & and then he is capable to enjoy his Estate Reall & personal I give him one Gunn

Item I give unto my Daughter Rebecca Bagwell free priveldge during her maidenhood to put upon my part of the Island any Creatures she is or may be possest w{i}^th all hereafter. I also give unto her one featherbed w[i]^th all furniture now belonging to it to be left in good condition as now it is when my said daughter attaine Seventeen years old and then she be capable to enjoy her Estate Reall & p[er]sonall I also give & bequeath to my said daughter one principal good Side Sadle fitt for a woman w[i]th all furniture that usually belongeth to a Side Saddle

Item Seven years that I have part of ye profit of my Mill with one Miller according to an agreemen^t between us made: I give that profit towards the maintenance of my wife and all my children And when seven years has expired if my saide wife continueth a widow So long she shall enjoy the profit of ^ye said Water Mill her part thereof And if she Remaineth not a widow then the benefit of my tow Sons & daughter for ever unto all their uses and every of their heirs for ever

Item All my houses & Land & Goods & Chattells w[ha]tsoever & Childrens male Cattell my will is that Ann Bagwell my wife shall Injoy ye use & benefit thereof my Son Henry & Alexander & my daughter Rebecca doth attained to their ages according to the above mentioned in this my will and my said shall enjoy and make use of all my hogs until then towards maintenance of her and all her children & and in case Ann my wife Remaineth a widow after my said children attainth to thir ages as above said soe long my Sais wife shall live up[on my land & and then have her choice of livelihood to live on ye said land. I also give my unto my said wife her choice of one of my horses for ever and I do give unto my said wife during her natuall life my negro boy & if in case my wife should depart this lIfe then the said Negro boy is to Remain for ever to the use to my daughter Rebeka Bagwell to her heirs & assigns for ever also my desire & will is that my Childrens Stocks and Chattels should Run together until they shall attaine to their respective ages above mentioned & then their Stocks to be deliverd them And my Children attaineth att age as abouves to have estates delivered & my will is that my Executors aforenamed lay out my Son Henry & my Son Alexander Bagwell Land at there ages being Eighteen years & deliver them there arts & then the said lands to Remaine to both Sons and their heies and Assigns for ever and likewise my will is that the Said Executrs deliver my said Daughter Rebeka Bagwell Estate to her of seventeen years old and then ye said Estate to remaine yo t^y use of hir & hir heirs & her heirs assignes for ever I also make my wife Ann Bagwell my sole Executrix & my Loveing Brother Thomas Bagwell & William Burton my Executrs in trust of this my Last Will and Testant upon condition that my said Executrix and both my Executrs pay all my Just debts.

I Revoking all other Wills and Testamts In witness whereas I have hereunto sett my hand & seal the day and year first above written

Signed Seal and delivered   *John Bagwell (the Seal)*

in presence of us   Novem^{ber} 30th 1686

Proved in open Court by ye Corporall oaths of *Isaac Metcalfe William Parker & Robt Watson* allowed of by ye Court and ordered to be recorded

Test Jno Washbourne Cl[erk] Cou[r]t

Recoreded Decem^{ber} 9th 1686

Appendix VI

Map of Virginia and Maryland, 1739

Early map showing the spread of English and Indian plantations, one of the earliest distributed maps to show Augustine Herman's landmark survey of Virginia, just after the time of Henry and Alice's grandchildren.

BIBLIOGRAPHY
List of Abbreviations

DCRS Devon and Cornwall Record Society
SWHT South West Heritage Trust

Archival Sources, Devon
Information at the Devon Heritage Centre, SWHT
Family Files

Chappell/Chapple
Gates family of East Devon
Jourdaine family of Exeter and Lyme Regis
Parr family
Raleigh family

Orphans' Court Inventories

David Bagwell, ECA Inventory, ECA 179.
Thomas Chappell, June 16, 1590, ECA Inventory 43 and National Archives, PROB 11/75/273.

Wills

Thomas Chappell, August 22, 1589, proved May 9, 1590. Original copy and transcript, Olive Moger Collection 8/36.
Thomazine Chappell, November 23, 1617, proved April 28, 1618, Moger Collection 1065–1067.
Devon Wills Index, 1163–1999, Transcriptions of Wills with Find My Past. www.findmypast.co.uk
Holman Bequest, a collection bequeathed by the Holman family of Topsham, involved in shipbuilding, and including logbooks dating from 1711 to 1895 (SWHT Z19/61/1–31).

Olive Moger Collection of wills, 1600–1800, Chappell Wills (x 929.3/MOG).

Church Records

Colyton Parish, Colyton, Part 1, Register of baptisms, marriages and deaths 1538–1837, transcribed and edited by A.J.P. Skinner, 1928 (DCRS).

St. Olave's Parish Records, transcribed by C.A.T. Fursdon and E. Serle, 1937 (DCRS).

St. Mary Arches Parish, Exeter, transcribed by C.A.T. Fursdon, 1926 (DCRS).

St. Mary's Church, Bideford. stmaryschurchbideford.org

St. Petrock's Parish, Exeter, Baptisms 1538–1812, Marriages 1538–1810, transcribed by Reverend F. Nesbitt (DCRS).

The Act Books (City and County of Exeter)

Hooker, John, *The Act Books* Vol. II to VIII (1508–1640).

Other Local Sources

Axe Valley Heritage Museum, Seaton, The Roy Chapple Collection, Bagwell and Chapple families.

www.seatonmuseum.co.uk

Colyton Heritage Centre: Bagwell Family files.

colytonheritagecentre.org

Layham Parish baptismal register, Ipswich and East Suffolk Record Office (ref no. FC 82).

Archival Sources, Virginia

The Library of Virginia: Archives Reference Services

Wills

John Bagwell, 1686, Part of index to Accomack County Wills and Administration (1663–1800), pp. 433a–434. Will pro November 30, 1686 (OS) December 9 (NS). Wills and Deeds, 1676–1690 (Reel 3).

Thomas Bagwell, 1690, Part of index to Accomack County Wills and Administration (1663–1800), pp. 525a–526a. Will pro September 16, 1690 and September 28, 1690. Wills and Deeds, 1676–1690 (Reel 3).

Patents

Visual Studies Collection Register, Land Patent, August 13, 1639. Source: Land Office Patents, No 1, 1623–1643 (v.1&2) p. 664 (Reel 1), Accomack County, Virginia System number 000718710.

Other sources

English Duplicates of Lost Virginia Records, compiled by Louise de Cognets, Junior, from records held on Virginias at the Public Records Office, London, 1958. Digitized by the University of Illinois, 2012.

Printed and digital sources

Allan, John, Alcock, Nat and Dawson, David, *West Country Households 1500–1700*, Monograph 9 (Woodbridge and New York, Society for Post-Medieval Archaeology, Boydell Press, 2015).

"America and West Indies: Addenda 1622." *Calendar of State Papers Colonial, America and West Indies*, Vol. 9, 1675–1676 and Addenda 1574–1674. British History Online. www.british-history.ac.uk

Ames, Susie M., "The Reunion of Two Virginia Counties," *Journal of Southern History*, Vol. 8, No. 4, Nov 1942, pp. 536–648.

Ames, Susie. M., *County Court Records of Accomack-Northampton, 1632–1640* (Washington, The American Historical Association, 1954).

Ames, Susie. M., *County Court Records of Accomack-Northampton, 1640–1645* (Charlottesville, VA, Virginia Historical Society, University Press of Virginia, 1973).

Ames, Susie. M., *Studies of the Eastern Shore in the Seventeenth Century* (New York, Russell and Russell, 1973).

Bernhard, Virginia, *A Tale of Two Colonies* (Columbia, SC, University of Missouri Press, 2011).

Billings, Warren M. (ed.), *The Old Dominion in the Seventeenth Century: A Documentary History of Virginia, 1606–1689* (Chapel Hill, NC, published for the Early American History and Culture, Williamsburg, VA, by the University of North Carolina Press, 1975).

Brazil, Robert Sean, "The Voyage and Wreck of the Sea Venture," 1609 Chronology. http://1609chronology.blogspot.com/2009/06/voyage-and-wreck-of-sea-venture.html

Breen, T.H. and Innes, Stephen, *"Myne Ground" Race and Freedom on Virginia's Eastern Shore, 1640–1676* (Oxford, Oxford University Press, 2005).

Brenner, Robert. *Merchants and Revolution* (London and New York, Verso, 2003).

Brock, R.A. (ed.) *Collections of the Virginia Historical Society: Abstracts of the Proceedings of the Virginia Company of London, 1619–1624*, Vol. 1. Prepared from Records in the Library of Congress by Conway Robinson (1968).

Bruce, Philip Alexander, *The Virginia Magazine of History and Biography*, ed. William G Stannard, Virginia Historical Society, Vol. XXV, 1917.

Burke's Genealogical and Heraldic History of the Landed Gentry, including American Families with British Ancestry (London, Burke's Peerage, 1939 [1826]).

Cann, William R., "Rev. William Cotton," Society of the Descendants of the Colonial Clergy.

https://www.colonialclergy.com/rev-william-cotton/

Charles Rivers Editors, *Jamestown* (Published by charlesriverseditors.com, Harvard and MIT).

Coldham, P.W. *The Complete Book of Emigrants, 1600–1660* (Baltimore, Genealogical Publishing Co.,1987).

Colyton Parish Through the Centuries (Devon, Colyton History Society, 2001).

Craven, Wesley Frank, *The Colonies in Transition 1660–1713* (New York, Harper and Rowe, 1968).

Craven, Wesley Frank, *The Virginia Company of London, Jamestown 350th Anniversary Historical Booklet*, No. 5 (Baltimore, MD, reprint for Clearfield Company by Genealogical Publishing Company, 2004).

Crocker, Jannine, *Elizabethan Inventories and Wills of Exeter's Orphans' Court*, Vol. 1 and 2 (Exeter, DCRS, 2016).

Cummings, Alex A. *Sir Francis Drake and the Golden Hind* (Norwich, Jarrold and Sons Ltd, 1987).

Curtis, Maggie, *Bideford Trade Maps*, with a foreword by Barry Hughes, North Devon Maritime Museum (Appledore, Devon, 2019).

Doherty, Kieran, *Sea Venture: Shipwreck, Survival and the Salvation of Jamestown* (New York, St. Martin's Press, 2007).

Dorman, John Frederick, *Adventurers of Purse and Person, Virginia, 1607–1624/5*, Vol. 1. Families A–F (Baltimore, Baltimore Genealogical Publishing Company Co, 4th edition, 2004).

Fleet, Beverley, *Virginia Colonial Abstracts, 1632–1637,* Vol. 1 (Clearfield Company, 2006).

Fry, E.A., *Calendars of Wills and Administrations Relating to the Counties of Devon and Cornwall* (Forgotten Books, 2017).

Glover, Lorri, "Sea Venture," Encylopedia Virginia. Virginia Foundation for the Humanities. https://www.encyclopediavirginia. org/Sea_Venture, 6 Dec 2012.

Heywood, Linda M. and Thornton, John K., *Central Africans, Atlantic Creoles, and the Foundation of the Americas, 1585–1660* (New York, Cambridge University Press, 2007).

Hickory House, *Exploring the Oldest Continuous Records of America* (Eastville, VA, Hickory House, 2007).

Horn, James, *A Land as God Made It: Jamestown and the Birth of America* (New York, Perseus Books Group, 2005).

Horn, James, *1619: Jamestown and the Forging of American Democracy* (New York, Basic Books, 2018).

The Hornbook of Virginia History, "Governors of Virginia," Encyclopedia Virginia. Virginia Foundation for the Humanities. www.encyclopediavirginia.org, January 25, 2018.

Hoskins W.G., *Old Devon* (London, David and Charles, 1966).

Hotton, James Camden (ed.), *The Original List of Persons of Quality — and Others who went from Great Britain to the American Plantations, 1600–1700* (New York, J.W. Bouton, 1874). Accessible on Ancestry.com.

Hutcheson, Virginia Lee, *Jamestowne Ancestors, 1606–1699* (Baltimore, MD, Genealogical Publishing Company, 2007).

Jefferson, Thomas, *Thomas Jefferson Papers*,1553–1599 and 1606–1827. Digital Collection, Library of Congress. https://www. loc.gov/collections/thomas-jefferson-papers/articles-and-essays/ virginia-records-timeline-115-to-1743/1553-to-1599y

Jourdaine, Sylvester. "Discovery of the Bermudas," in *A Voyage to Virginia in 1609, Two Narratives*. Edited by Louis B. Wright (Charlottesville and London, University of Virginia Press, 2nd edition, 2013).

Kelly, Joseph, *Marooned: Jamestown, Shipwreck, and a New History of America's Origin* (New York, Bloomsbury, 2018).

Kelso, William M., *Jamestown: The Buried Truth* (Charlottesville, VA, University of Virginia Press, 2006).

Kelso, William M., *Jamestown, The Truth Revealed* (Charlottesville, VA, University of Virginia Press, 2017).

Kingsbury, Susan Myra (ed.), *The Records of the Virginia Company of London*, The Court Books, 1619–1622, Vol. I (Heritage Books, 2009 [1906]).

Kingsbury, Susan Myra (ed.), *The Records of the Virginia Company of London*, The Court Books, 1622–1624, Vol. II (Heritage Books, 2009 [1906]).

Kingsbury, Susan Myra (ed.), *The Records of the Virginia Company of London*, Documents 1, 1607–1622, Vol. III (Heritage Books, 2010 [1933]).

Kingsbury, Susan Myra (ed.), *The Records of the Virginia Company of London*, Documents 2, 1623–1626, Vol. IV (Heritage Books, 2009 [1935]).

Kolb, Avery, "The Tempest," *American Heritage*, Vol. 34, No. 2, April/May 1983.

Look Bermuda/Look Films, *Downing's Wreck—The Story of the Sea Venture*. https://www.lookbermuda.com/seaventure

McCartney, Martha. W., *Virginia Immigrants and Adventurers, 1607–1635* (Baltimore, Genealogical Publishing Company, 2007).

McCurdy, Mary, "The English Origins and History of Henry Bagwell and Thomas Stratton on the Early Eastern Shore of

Virginia," *The Virginia Genealogists*, Vol. 30, No. 1, Jan. 1986, pp. 3–16.

Mackay, Dr. Howard and Groves, Marlene A. (eds.), *Northampton County, Virginia Record Book, Court Cases, Vol. 8, 1657–1664* (Maine, Picton Press, 2002).

Mackay, Dr. Howard, Groves, Marlene A., and Hinkley, Alma (eds.), *Northampton County, Virginia Record Book Orders, Deeds and Wills, Vol. 5, 1654–1655* (Maine, Picton Press, 1999).

Marshall, James Handley (ed.), *Abstracts of the Wills and Administrations of Northampton County, Virginia, 1632–1802* (New England History Press, 1994).

Neill, Edward D., *History of the Virginia Company of London* (New York, Joel Munsell, 1869).

Nicholls, Mark, and Williams, Penry. *Sir Walter Raleigh: In Life and Legend* (London, Bloomsbury, 2011).

Nottingham, Stratton, *Accomack County Court Orders and Administrations, 1663–1680* (Bowie, Maryland, Heritage Books, 1990).

Nottingham, Stratton (ed.), *Wills and Administrations of Accomack County, Virginia 1663–1800* (Genealogical Co., Baltimore, 1999 [1931]).

Nugent, N. Marion, *Cavaliers and Pioneers, Abstracts of Virginia Land Patents and Grants, 1623–1666*, Vol. 1 (Richmond, VA, Patent Books, 1934). University of Illinois Library, 333.3 N894c vi. Digitized by Internet Archives 2012.

"Old Blackwall." *Survey of London: Poplar, Blackwall and Isle of Dogs*, Vols 43 and 44. Ed. Hermione Hobhouse (London: London County Council, 1994). British History Online. https://www.british-history.ac.uk/survey-london/vols43-4/pp548-552

Oliver, Reverend George, *The History of the City of Exeter* (Exeter, William Roberts, 1861).

Perry, James. R., *Formation of a Society on Virginia's Eastern Shore, 1615–1655* (Chapel Hill, NC, and London, University of North Carolina Press, 1990).

Porter, Charles W. III, *Adventurers to a New World, The Roanoke Colony, 1585–87* (Washington, National Park Service, 1972).

Quinn, David. B and Quinn, Alison M. (eds.), *The First Colonists* (North Carolina, Archives and History, North Carolina Department of Cultural Resources, 2007).

Raine, David F., *Sir George Somers, A Man of his Times* (Bermuda, Pompano Publications, 1994).

Rice, Douglas Walthew, *The Life and Achievements of Sir John Popham, 1531–1607* (Cranbury, Rosemont Publishing and Printing Group, 2005).

Rogers, Inkerman, *A Concise History of Bideford, AD 878–1936* (Bideford, 1938).

Rowe, Margery, M. (ed.), *Tudor Exeter, Tax assessments, 1489–1595, including the Military Survey, 1522* (Exeter, DCRS, New Series, Vol. 2, 1977).

Rowe, Margery M. and Jackson, Andrew M., *Exeter Freemen, 1266–1967, Mayor's Court Book 55* (Exeter, DCRS, Extra Series, No. 1, 1973).

Salmon, Emily Jones and Salmon, John, "Tobacco in Colonial Virginia," *Encyclopedia Virginia*. Virginia Foundation for the Humanities. www.encyclopediavirginia.org

Spurling, Rick, "Tobacco: The Intriguing Story of Bermuda and Virginia," www.royalgazette.com/article/20120430/ISLAND/704309994, April 30, 2012.

Strachey, William. "A True Reportory of the Wreck and Redemption of Sir Thomas Gates," in *A Voyage to Virginia in 1609, Two Narratives*. Edited by Louis B. Wright (Charlottesville and London, University of Virginia Press, 2nd edition, 2013).

Stratton, Harriet Russell, *Book of Strattons*, Vol. 1 (New York, The Grafton Press, 1908).

Turman, Nora Miller. *The Eastern Shore of Virginia, 1603–1694* (Maryland, Heritage Books, 2007).

United States Department of Interior, Heritage and Conservation and Recreation Service, *National Register of Historic Places Inventory; Stratton Manor*. Original date registered, 1940; Inventory 1958 (November 11, 1980).

Walker, R.F., *Transcriptions from Colonial Records of Virginia*, State Paper Office, Vol. 3, No. 2 (Archives).

Walczyk, Frank V., *Northampton County, Virginia, Orders, Deeds & Wills 1651–1654*, Vol. IV (Coram, NY, Petersrow, 1999).

Whitelaw, Ralph Thomas, *Virginia's Eastern Shore*, Vols I and II (Virginia Historical Society, 1951).

Wilheit, M.C., "Obedience Robins of Accomack: 17th Century Strategies for Success," MA Thesis, Texas A&M University, submitted December 1997.

Willard, Fred, "Trade Items as Transfer of Money." http://www.lost-colony.com/trade.html

Wingood, Allan J., "*Sea Venture*: An Interim Report of an Early 17th Century Shipwreck Lost in 1609," *International Journal of Nautical Archaeology and Underwater Exploration*, 1982, 11(4), pp. 333–337.

Wise, Jennings Cropper, *Ye Kingdome of Accawmacke or the Eastern Shore of Virginia in the Seventeenth Century* (Clearfield, 1967 [1911]).

Wooley, Benjamin, *Savage Kingdom: The True Story of Jamestown 1607 and the Settlement of America* (New York, Harper Collins, 2007).

Wright, Louis B. (ed.), *A Voyage to Virginia in 1609, Two Narratives* (Charlottesville and London, University of Virginia Press, 2nd edition, 2013).

Websites with a membership fee

Ancestry. www.ancestry.com
Find my Past. www.findmypast.co.uk
Georgia Pioneers. georgiapioneers.com

Useful websites for Devon history

Devon Heritage Centre. swheritage.org.uk
Exeter Memories. www.exetermemories.co.uk
The National Archives. www.national archives.gov.uk.
Tuckers Hall. www.tuckershall.org.uk

Useful websites for Bermuda history

Bermuda and her Atlantic Islands. www.bermuda-online.org
St. George's Foundation. www.stgeorgesfoundation.org

Useful websites for Virginia history

2019 Commemoration. www.historyisfun.org
Bayside Transcriptions. baysidetranscriptions@gmail.com.
Department of Historic Resources. www.dhr.virginia.gov
Eastern Shore Public Library. www.shorelibrary.com
Eastern Shore of Virginia Historical Society.
collections@shorehistory.org.
Find a Grave. www.findagrave.com
First Colony Foundation. www.firstcolonyfoundation.org
Fort Raleigh National Historic Park, North Carolina. www.nps.gov
Genealogy and History of the Eastern Shore. www.esva.net/ghotes.
Governors of Virginia. www.encyclopediavirginia.org
Hampton History Museum. https://hampton.gov/119/Hampton-History-Museum

History of Jamestown. Historic Jamestown, Part of Colonial Natural Historic Park. https://www.nps.gov/jame/learn/historyculture/a-short-history-of-jamestown.htm

Jamestown Rediscovery Foundation and Preservation Virginia. www.historicjamestowne.org

Jamestowne Society, Richmond. www.jamestowne.org

Library of Virginia, Archives Reference Services. www.lva.virginia.gov

Markers of Virginia. www.hmdb.org

Miles, Barry and Miles, M.K., *Miles Files*, Virginia Eastern Shore Library, Accomack. http://espl-genealogy.org/MilesFiles/site/index.htm

Native Americans in Accomack, Virginia. www.nativeamericansofdelawarestate.com

Northampton Historic Preservation Society. nhps100@gmail.com.

Order of Descendants of Ancient Planters. www.ancientplanters.org

Powhatan Indian World (US National Park Service). www.nps.gov/jame/learn/historyculture/chronology-of-powhatan-indian-activity.htm

Tobacco. archive.tobacco.org

Virginia Department of Historic Resources. www.dhr.virginia.gov

Virginia Eastern Shore Public Library. www.shorelibrary.com

Virginia Records Timeline 1553 to 1743. https://www.loc.gov/collections/thomas-jefferson-papers/articles-and-essays/virginia-records-timeline-1553-to-1743/

Virtual Jamestown. www.virtualjamestown.org

Wikitree.com, Henry Bagwell entry managed by Chet Snow. www.wikitree.com/wiki/Bagwell-209

ACKNOWLEDGMENTS

I would like to thank the following people who have helped me to bring Henry Bagwell's story into the world and celebrate his journey from Devon to Virginia, in the exciting world of the early 1600s and the colonization of America.

It has taken many years but the staff at the Devon Heritage Centre, Exeter, must be commended for their patience when asked to locate many unusual documents and files on Devon's people and places.

My research had taken me to other smaller Heritage Centres, in particular the Colyton Heritage Centre, where the late John Cochrane shared his knowledge of the Bagwell family and advised me of the late Roy Chapple collection on families at the Axe Valley Heritage in Seaton.

Two friends, David Meredith and Pat Paynter, in our local University of the Third Age (U3A) History Group, read through the original script and made comment.

Dr. Mark Nicholls, Postgraduate tutor and college lecturer in History, Librarian and former President of St. John's College, Cambridge, and author of *Sir Walter Raleigh, In Life and Legend*, kindly reviewed the first manuscript and offered excellent advice. This resulted in my own review of the content and the separation of the manuscript into two books, one the story of *The Chappell Family, Merchants and Mayors of Exeter*, and the other this volume, *The Henry Bagwell Story*.

Dr. George Cook, Bermuda historian, retired president of Bermuda College, provided additional information on aspects of the *Sea Venture* story.

The staff of the Library of Virginia Archives gave advice on searching the land patents in the Eastern Shore; thanks also to Susie

B. Sample, Assistant Clerk at the Circuit Court for Northampton County, Eastville, Virginia, for her continued support with information, and to the amazing resource and research of M.K. Miles, genealogist and author of family histories of people of the Eastern Shore and his website called Miles Files.

David Scott, Northampton Historic Preservation Society, gave his support and provided the images of Stratton Manor, its Marker and Northampton County Court House.

My thanks to Jane Simmonds, whose skill and expertise in editing the script has contributed to the style of the book and whose eyes do not miss the smallest of mistakes.

Thanks also to my brother Kenneth R. Maxwell, author and historian, who has supported me with every step, with reading and rereading chapters and offering advice and critical analysis. I thank my husband Ray for his endless help with computer expertise, patience in assisting with alterations to texts, photographs, and accompanying me to churches and churchyards. My son Andrew and daughter Nicola showed constant support and interest in Henry's story.

Finally to my parents, the late Kenneth and Jean Maxwell, who imbued in me a love of history and confidence in myself to achieve, and my uncle Victor Maxwell, who started his own journey into family history in the early 1960s. I inherited his notebooks and in them was the beginning of this story.

Their mother and my grandmother was Mary Ann Hearn Chapple (February 8, 1874 to May 1, 1967).

INDEX

W

Y